Life Skills for a Broken World

Dr Ahona Guha is a clinical and forensic psychologist from Melbourne, Australia. She works with victims of abuse and trauma, and clients with a range of other difficulties — such as anxiety, depression, perfectionism, burnout, and relationship problems. She also works with perpetrators of harmful behaviours to assess risk, and provides treatment to reduce the risk they pose to others. She writes widely for the media on matters related to mental health, health, social justice, and equity. Her work has appeared in *The Age*, *The Guardian*, *The Saturday Paper*, *Breathe Magazine*, and on SBS and ABC. You can find out more about her work at **ahonaguha.com**.

Life
Skills
for a
Broken
World

Dr Ahona Guha

illustrations by Angi Thomas

SCRIBE

Melbourne • London

Scribe Publications
18–20 Edward St, Brunswick, Victoria 3056, Australia
2 John St, Clerkenwell, London, WC1N 2ES, United Kingdom
3754 Pleasant Ave, Suite 100, Minneapolis, Minnesota 55409, USA

Published by Scribe 2024

Typeset in Adobe Caslon Pro by the publishers

Printed and bound in China by R.R. Donnelley

Scribe is committed to the sustainable use of natural resources and
the use of paper products made responsibly from those resources.

Scribe acknowledges Australia's First Nations peoples as the
traditional owners and custodians of this country, and we
pay our respects to their elders, past and present.

978 1 922585 95 0 (Australian edition)
978 1 914484 93 3 (UK edition)
978 1 957363 58 5 (US edition)
978 1 761385 50 6 (ebook)

Catalogue records for this book are available from the
National Library of Australia and the British Library.

scribepublications.com.au
scribepublications.co.uk
scribepublications.com

For Karla, my best girl
&
For Snigdha and Steph —
(close) second best girls.

Contents

There are two ways you can use this book.

First, reading it from start to finish. This is my preferred method because it means you will understand the framework for living that I present and will be able to see how the pieces of the puzzle fit together. This is a good place to start if you are generally feeling okay, are curious about yourself and the world, and want to find ways to keep feeling okay.

Second, if you're not feeling great, you may want to dip in and out and focus on the skills that appeal to your situation. If you do this, it may still be good to go back and read the rest of the book when you feel up to it. The table of contents provides a list of the skills covered, so you can choose a pathway that works for you.

It's important to remember that this book is not a replacement for therapy or mental health assistance; but it is something you can use as a support in conjunction with professional care.

Before we launch into things, a caveat. While I do work for a public mental health service, all views in this book are my own only.

Introduction

At age 23, I found myself divorced, and reeling in the knowledge that my life had taken a catastrophic turn. I'd been raised in a 'good' family. On the outside, my childhood looked normal. I received many of the things one expects — a good education, support, warmth, and shelter. I was expected to do well, to live a normal life, and have the things people typically hope for: degrees, a satisfying job, achievement, maybe a family.

But my 'good' family was beset by intergenerational trauma and undiagnosed mental health difficulties — with all the attendant difficulties that come when these things occur unrecognised. So on the inside, things were a little different. I carried an unseen burden of trauma, and happiness felt far from my grasp. I didn't know how to approach the world; I was unmoored and drifting. I had no close relationships, poor self-esteem, and little understanding of emotion — mine or others. I grabbed at whatever offered me a semblance of meaning, protection, or belonging — which is how I found myself in a doomsday cult at 17, engaged at 19, and a university dropout and married at 20.

When I left both the cult and my marriage at 23, I had nothing. I lived thousands of kilometres away from family, had few friends and little money, and had no education to fall back on. I also had psychological devastation to manage — early and more recent traumas, and serious depression as I sifted through the wreck of my life. I re-entered the world after spending years being told that it was about to end, and that I was going to hell for eternity unless I spent my time cartwheeling through a range of acts to save my soul. This left me with a peculiar kind of apathy ('What even matters if we are all going to hell?'), angst, and severe anxiety when I started to return to the world.

Luckily, I found my way into some excellent therapy. I made some friends, I got a job I liked, and I started studying psychology. I wanted to eke out whatever meaning and joy I could from life, after years spent frozen.

I didn't know it then, but these simple steps, my dual focus on meaning and joy, and the framework I started to build for myself saved me and helped me establish the life I have now, which I love. A life that is much bigger than the suffering I once endured but which is nevertheless built on my acknowledgement of that suffering, and the strength, courage, and self-compassion it took me to climb past it. The sorrows I experienced forced me to confront some very dark things, which, in turn, allowed me to think deeply about the world and to determine what would help me build a life worth living; even (and especially) when it was hard. I built a framework for living — a set of skills and practices and a considered orientation towards certain values that supported me as I worked towards a meaningful life. This framework carried me through, and it's one I share with you in this book, as together we explore ways to survive and thrive in these difficult times.

* * *

It's no exaggeration to say that the world feels very difficult right now — perhaps like it's broken, even, with humanity racing towards some form of collapse. There have been several large shifts in the geopolitical order, including the rise of a strong far-right movement and various forms of ideologically driven terrorism. Despots, dictators, or the ineffectual and bumbling have assumed political power in many countries and the average, everyday citizen (i.e., you and me) may be feeling helpless, hopeless, and despairing. Hard-won women's rights are being decimated globally, including the right to have control over one's own body. Costs of living are spiralling, locking many people out of achieving basic goals, like home and food security. Climate change is a reality we can no longer avoid. We have survived one pandemic, with zoonosis likely to contribute to other pandemics arising within our lifetime.

The question for most of us might be — how do I live through these times and hold onto hope, both for myself and for the future of the world?

Apart from big events, like a pandemic, most of us carry burdens that feel unique to us — yet many of these burdens are also universal. Broken hearts, sadness, anger, anxieties, worries, regrets, big feelings, illness, unwanted life changes, isolation and loneliness, trauma — it is guaranteed that each of us will experience at least some of these over the course of a well-lived human life. Some of us will integrate this life pain into our experiences, but many of us will struggle to make sense of it and may become stuck in widening loops of emotional pain and questioning. *Why? Why me? Why now?*

3

Psychologically, too, the world feels like a dangerous place. Violence is common, conversation is polarised, with little tolerance of dissenting views, and the world is riskier, with people banding into tight-knit communities and excluding others. Bullying and harassment are rife; some social groups are treated very poorly, while others hold power and resources. We have learnt to numb ourselves to this by acquiring things or sinking into mindless entertainment. We self-soothe and we self-stimulate; anything to ensure we don't feel.

While many of us, especially in the West, were raised to believe that we can and should have it all, the world has changed such that this may no longer be possible (and to be fair, it never truly was). Many of us feel socially disconnected but virtually hyper-connected; we're stressed, burnt out, anxious, sad, and hopeless. We are physically more comfortable than we've ever been, but psychologically tortured. Many of us are struggling with mental health, and don't understand why.

In these difficult times, it is important to have a good framework for living. And to build one, we need to think about our assumptions of the world and the ways in which we manage our lives. We need a deep understanding of the underlying factors that allow us to appreciate the colour in life: real social connections, emotional wellbeing, realistic expectations of what life is likely to offer, some acceptance of the inevitability of distress, and the capacity to question our own thinking. We need to find meaning that encompasses more than acquiring things or finding pleasure, and to recognise what we truly value and why we value the things we do.

People who have a strong framework for living are better able to make sense of hard times. During the pandemic, this meant that some people could put in place simple actions, like planning regular walks with friends during lockdowns instead of the dinners and other social activities that were common pre-pandemic, and could understand why these behaviours helped: i.e., exercise releases endorphins, and establishing meaningful routines that control things within one's sphere and letting go of the rest are powerful psychological tools. So, too, is the ability to keep in mind that the lockdowns were put in place to protect each other.

Making conscious choices about living, according to a broader framework, stood people in much better stead than those who tried to enact certain behaviours without really understanding what they were feeling, why they were feeling as they were, or how to soothe those emotions. Building and living according to a meaningful framework helps us cope with specific mental health issues, and can be beneficial for anyone who finds life difficult or tedious at times.

The set of skills and practices that make up the framework I present in this book are ones I built up slowly, over a decade of personal therapy, psychology study, and research. I continue to draw on these skills and insights, and they support me as I navigate the swings and roundabouts of human life, with all its joys, sorrows, and attendant fluctuations. This framework is not built on avoidance of distress, but rather is designed to help us notice it, name it, understand it, and soothe it. It incorporates a range of psychological skills, based on broader philosophical and psychological practices and research. It is designed to help us understand and live through difficult times and in a broken world.

What I present to you here is a secular framework. I no longer have a personal faith. In many ways, this has made things more difficult for me, as I haven't had the easy access to inbuilt meaning that comes with religious belief. In other ways, it's made me even more determined to find meaning for myself and to think about what it is that makes my life here on earth worth living. I believe that it's also made me more compassionate and tolerant, as I can't mine religion for answers (or defences) to human conundrums, but must instead try to offer a human response, and human care.

It is also a political framework. It feels only fair to warn you of this at the outset. I don't attempt to tell you how to align yourself politically or who to vote for, but I do talk about the importance of matters such as equity, resisting and protesting harmful things, and understanding disinformation. Many of these issues are inherently political in nature, given our economic and social structures. The issues causing us so much distress come from the sociopolitical spaces we have built, and finding a way to be okay in the world will often involve changing these spaces, or our use of these spaces, in some way.

This is a book of understanding, of action, of realism, of anti-hustle, and some tolerable discomfort — not a pastel book of self-care, bubble baths, motivational quotes, and polite platitudes.

However, it is also a book of joy and pleasure. Being open to the enjoyment of living in a body and having a beautiful world to explore is central in anchoring ourselves against pain. Appreciating qualities like hope, humour, social connection, pleasure, novelty, and joy is essential. Embrace the bubble baths — and the glitter, apple pies, good sex, hiking, skydiving, travel, learning, slow stacks of books, crunch of toast, autumn nip, summer sun. Find your body, find your adventure; and find some joy to bookmark the hard parts. Being alive is a pretty miraculous thing, when we think of the primordial soup we all came from.

Although the world feels grim, I'm still hopeful for our future. Human endeavours move in cycles, over time, and while there is much darkness in the world, those of us reading this book are freer than ever to talk about, name, and hopefully challenge that darkness. There are pockets of community-level change across the world, and millions of people are taking personal and political stands for a better future. We are more invested in fairness and kindness than ever before.

We are awake to how we have been breaking the world.

Both America (in 2020) and Australia (in 2022) voted out despotic, disinterested, and cruel governments, paving the way for people (and policy platforms) invested in intelligent thinking, climate change activism, and visions of equity, fairness, and hope. These movements are large and powerful but will require sustained effort, commitment, and the psychological skills needed to manage ourselves and each other as we make big shifts in how we live, with the discomfort and opposition that these will surely bring.

Fred Rogers coined the phrase 'Look for the helpers' as a tool for parents who were trying to help their children cope with news of disasters. This can be a revitalising and hope-inspiring mindset for all. We need to look to the darkness to understand it, but we also need to turn to the people dashing towards the darkness, bringing some light; and then, ideally, we can be these people ourselves. To do so, though, we need a framework that helps us understand and tolerate difficult times, and supports us to hold fast with targeted, meaningful action.

I hope that this book can provide you with such a framework.

Building your framework

Before we can plunge into learning skills and techniques, we need to understand some basics about mental health, including the difference between mental health and mental illness, some ways to improve mental health, the differences between emotions and thoughts, and our main values (and why they are important).

This section will help us form an understanding of these basics and give us a range of skills we can use to start building our mental health and wellbeing from the ground up.

The basics of mental health

It's very hard to manage difficulties, or understand them, without a basic 'framework for life' in place. Think of this as you would the frame of a house — without it, we might manage to build a house of sorts, but it will likely be fragile and crooked, with large gaps that allow draughts, and a collapsing roof. It will provide some shelter but may not withstand a storm.

> Having a framework for life won't take away distress, but does mean that when distress comes, we will be able to understand it and decide how to manage it.

A framework for life is made up of a sound understanding of what mental health is, realistic expectations about life, and good relationships — the knowledge of how to form them and how to maintain them. Psychologists call these things 'social and emotional capital'; the more skills we possess in our emotional bank accounts, the richer our experience of the world is likely to be. As with real bank accounts, attributes we place in this bank account grow over time (with practice) and can be used as buffers for a rainy day, or to support us with the demands of daily living. Interest compounds, and the more we practise these skills, the stronger our mental health will become over time.

Satisfying basic needs first

This book is largely concerned with building the skills to ensure mental health after our most basic needs are met, but it is important to mention these needs first, as without them, the rest is moot.

> If we cannot satisfy our basic needs for food, warmth, shelter, safety, and health, it is difficult to focus on bigger-picture things such as building social connections or values-aligned living.

I often use Maslow's hierarchy of needs when thinking of mental wellbeing.

I begin by stressing the importance of the social context we live in — and issues like equitable and socialised health-care, the right to bodily autonomy, and basic income. I do this for a reason. Without these things, none of us will be able to achieve true mental health.

Once we have satisfied these basic needs, we can focus on building social connections and closeness. Questions at this stage might include: How do we find friends we feel safe with? Or, how do we find a good partner? Finally, we approach the top of the pyramid — self-actualisation. This step includes focusing on even broader issues, such as our need to learn and grow, our desire to find beauty in the world, and ways to live a meaningful life. For true mental health, for ourselves and others, we need to work towards social and political structures that help us build the base of the pyramid — for everyone.

What is mental health?

The phrase 'mental health' is often used as shorthand for being okay all the time, but this eradicates and collapses the beautiful complexities and the nuanced emotion that life can bring. We can't feel good all the time — our brains just aren't set up that way. True mental health means understanding this and being able to accept the difficulties in life, and find some meaning through them.

From a neurobiological perspective, all our emotions carry information — they're a sense we use to navigate in the world. Disgust tells us that something is rotten and could kill or hurt us; anxiety tells us there may be danger; guilt signals we have done something wrong and need to make reparations to be part of our social group again. All these emotions come and go based on external and internal cues, and without experiencing the so-called 'negative' feelings, we would lose information about the world and our role in it.

It's important here to separate the concept of mental illness from mental health. Mental illness refers to diagnosable mental health conditions (such as post-traumatic stress disorder, generalised anxiety disorder, schizophrenia) that come with big changes in how one may think, feel, and perceive the world. This book explores a range of concepts around mental health, but it doesn't address recovery from specific mental illnesses. People who struggle with mental illness may also find value in the book, as the skills I talk about apply to good mental health for all, but it's important to remember that mental illnesses require additional specific and targeted treatment, such as therapy and/or medication.

Mental health is a much broader concept and means psychological, emotional, and social wellbeing, as well as concepts such as finding meaning and happiness, managing stress, and building connection. Mental health can be seen as a continuum, from poor and struggling with specific difficulties, to okay, to thriving and flourishing. Mental health is not just the *absence* of mental illness but also includes concepts such as rich relationships, meaning-making, psychological flexibility, joy, play, and resilience.

Checking in on your mental health
Most people will slide along this spectrum at different times, and it's helpful to check in often and ask yourself how your mental health is going.

- Do you have any specific difficulties (e.g., lack of good relationships, or anxiety) or diagnosed mental health disorders that have not yet been treated?
  If yes, seeking treatment should be a priority.
- Do you feel safe and connected?
- Do you have meaningful work that pays enough to live on?
- Can you accept, and tolerate, a range of emotions?
- Are you caring for your body?
- Do you rest enough? If not, what gets in the way of rest?
- Do you have friends? Do you feel supported by them?
- Are you able to play (whatever that looks like) and have some fun?
- Are you satisfied with your goals, and do you feel like you can effect change in your life?
- Do you feel okay about yourself, and content with your life?
- Can you accept imperfection and mistakes?

These questions may seem simple, but they're important. If you notice a lack in any areas, you can start to problem-solve.

If you identify a lack in one of these areas, what is one small step you can take next week towards filling this gap? Mental health does not just arrive at our doorstep, we must build it actively each day.

Practical steps towards basic mental health
When I focus on the basics of mental health with clients, I work on building the following:

- *Sleep* — ideally, seven to eight hours a day. Without sleep, our brains are as if intoxicated, and we won't be able to feel good, or think and reason well.
- *Food* — eating three simple meals a day (make them complex if you want, of course! I am just encouraging the basics to keep it easy) and snacks. Forget superfoods or eating 'clean' (a ridiculous concept that has no grounding in nutritional science) — anything fresh and relatively unprocessed is all your body needs. Without food, your blood sugar will fluctuate, and your mood will be more difficult to manage. Your body needs to eat. Nothing looks as good as well-nourished *feels*.
- *Exercise* — move your body. Start small, a few minutes of whatever form of movement or stretching you can manage — but move. Some is better than none, more is better than some. Find something you like doing — you don't have to run, do a HIIT class, exercise for an hour for benefits. Mix it up. Do it even if you don't want to — waiting for motivation can sometimes mean waiting for a long time. Focus on the benefits for health, not on shifting your weight or changing your body size. As always, pacing is important, so if you have a disability or chronic illness, please pay close attention to your body and what it can tolerate each day.
- *Structure and routine* — lying in bed and watching Netflix all day will destroy your mood, and leave you feeling bored, apathetic, and isolated. We all need rest days, and it's absolutely fine to do this sometimes, but a good daily routine, with a mix of activity/work/ exercise/social connection, will help you to feel okay about yourself.

- *Connection* — connection with people we care about is important, whatever form it takes. A hug from a family member, a chat with a friend, a bookclub meeting. Online connections can be part of this but are not a full replacement for face-to-face connections.
- *Pleasure* — when things feel grim, we can use pleasurable activities as a hot air balloon to lift us up, up and away. This includes things that feel good to you (e.g., massages, time with friends, a nice meal, sunshine) and things that can make you feel you have a sense of mastery or are improving your skills (working on a personal best as a runner, reading a new book, learning a new language).

Break down bigger goals into small, achievable steps

- If you are currently struggling with mental health, which of the above do you need to work on?
- How will you do this?
- What's the first step?
- What supports and resources might you need?

Mental health myth busting

We are taught a range of myths about mental health and wellness, which means we often flounder and struggle to recognise the things we can do to proactively address how we feel. At their base, all mental health disorders involve difficulties managing emotion and thinking. Learning to understand and manage how we feel and think helps us recover from (or prevent) these difficulties.

In the course of my work, and in my day-to-day life, here are some of the more common myths I have encountered:

- Any distress is problematic.
- Pain and sadness should be avoided at all costs.
- Difficult emotions need to be 'managed' or 'processed' neatly (i.e., reduced).
- Emotions should be pushed away.
- Or, conversely, all emotions need to be expressed and validated all the time.
- Our thoughts always reflect reality.
- Our memories are a perfect record of what happened.
- Our relationships must always fulfil us.
- If we try hard enough, we can achieve anything.
- How we feel comes from within — with no social or outside influences at all.

On the surface, some of these beliefs are okay. For instance, if we believe that if we try hard and practise, we can learn new things and achieve goals, we will likely have a greater sense of self-efficacy (the belief that we can effect change and influence our lives) than if we feel that our skills and talents are predetermined. However, even these helpful mindsets can be taken too far, especially when connected with hustle and productivity culture.

The last myth in the list is particularly destructive.

> We often ignore the reality of social influences, holding instead a hyper-individualistic view, but the societal structures we live in contribute enormously to our mental health, and it can help us to recognise this when we are struggling. While we do need to cultivate our own resilience (the capacity to bounce back from difficult circumstances), wellbeing is strongly influenced by the structures around us, such as work demands and social-security systems.

As you read this book, there are some mental health myths I'd like you to think about — and then drop.

> **Myth:** Mental health means I do not feel sad, angry, anxious, distressed, or upset.
> **Truth:** Mental health means that you understand and allow for *all* emotions, seeing them as *responses* to the world and *information* for you about how to live your life and what is and isn't working. The human brain is wired to feel all these emotions at various times — they all provide necessary information, and they can't be pushed away.

Myth: Once I fix my mental health, I will never have a bad day/week.
Truth: Living a thinking and feeling life means you *will* sometimes have bad days or weeks. Having good mental health means you understand, examine, allow, and usefully respond to these difficult times, instead of panicking and pushing them away — or giving in to them completely.

Myth: I need to fix my mental health before I do X, Y, or Z.
Truth: Putting off life because of poor mental health is likely contributing to keeping you stuck. Do as many of the things you want as you can, despite how you feel, and you may find that your mental health improves as a result.

Myth: My mental health is bad because of my childhood/relationship/history, and I can't fix it.
Truth: While your mental health might be poor because of things that happened to you (traumas, upbringing, and genetics all contribute to mental health difficulties), you have a responsibility to yourself to work on finding healing. It may be difficult to understand why other people have hurt you, and hard to accept that the only person who can help you find recovery is yourself — but it's also essential for wellbeing and for living a good life.

Myth: I can't be mentally well until I do X, Y, and Z — for example, find a partner/have a child/finish my degree.
Truth: None of these things will bring you mental health or wellbeing. True wellbeing sits outside what you possess/have/engage in, and you can work on understanding and building wellbeing even when you feel things are missing from your life. Of course, it's important to feel that you are working towards the things you want and that you have a meaningful life, so taking steps to achieve cherished goals is important, but it's helpful to focus on the process and your actions — not just the outcome.

Myth: I don't have time to work on being okay.
Truth: If you don't make time for wellness now, you'll probably need to make time for illness later. This goes for both physical and mental health.

Myth: Mental health is about feeling happy.
Truth: Happiness is just one emotion. You will sometimes feel happy, just as you will sometimes feel other emotions (love, sadness, rage, anxiety, fear, greed, disgust, etc.). Feeling one emotion can't be your ultimate goal, and we all have a biologically determined happiness set-point, making constant efforts to be happier pointless (it's a little like trying to raise your body's natural temperature set-point, or change its alkalinity.) Researchers have studied this at length and found that most people fluctuate within a small range of happiness. It's possible to influence this to some extent — for example, committed political and social action and connection have been found to improve wellbeing, whereas focus on career gains and material goals are detrimental. Similarly, big events such as divorce or an acquired disability can reduce wellbeing. However, trying to artificially force happiness is unlikely to pay off. You will sometimes feel happy if you do meaningful things, find purpose and connection, and have a sustainable lifestyle — but this is a by-product of the process, not the goal itself. Mental health is more closely connected to finding *meaning*, than to finding happiness.

Myth: I don't care about other people; I just want to feel okay within myself.

Truth: You will never feel truly okay in a world beset by inequality, nastiness, and poor distribution of resources. The world is connected in many ways, and things that might feel distant currently (such as climate change, geopolitical conflict, or economic policy) will inevitably come to affect your life. Filling your own cup first is important, but a mentally healthy and meaningful life inevitably requires social connections and contribution to the wellbeing of other people. Exclusively tending to your own thoughts, feelings, and wants won't create the broader social conditions all humans need to have a good life. Equally, ignoring your own needs and only giving to other people will also leave you unhappy and stressed.

Do you believe any of these myths? If yes, how does this play out in how you live your life? And what is one simple step you can take to move away from it?

FURTHER READING

The New Rulebook — Chris Cheers

An excellent book by a psychologist presenting a new way of living, focused on community, acceptance, and care.

Why Has Nobody Told Me This Before — Dr Julie Smith

An evidence-based exploration of mental health, with realistic and helpful tools and tips provided by a clinical psychologist.

Making meaning

Most approaches in psychology focus on the need to find meaning as essential for human happiness and growth. Most of the bigger questions we ask ourselves (Why am I here? What is the purpose of my life?) have no definite answers, but they can be explored through the concept of *meaning*.

In the past, religion has often provided these answers, but as our societies become increasingly secular, many of us need to work a little harder to define our own meaning.

Meaning involves defining how to best live your life, so that it is in pursuit of the qualities and ethics you most deeply value.

This will be unique to each of us, but finding or constructing a framework of meaning can guide all our actions.

Meaning rather than happiness

Humans need to focus on something other than ourselves and our own needs, whatever this *something* might be. Making meaning allows us to focus on things bigger than just trying to find happiness. A search for happiness usually won't bear fruit unless we can extend this search to finding meaning as well. Happiness will come and go; meaning is longer-term and helps us tolerate suffering as we work towards things we care about.

When I work with clients who are suicidal or despairing, a lack of meaning in life is one of the biggest factors driving this ideation. We all need to feel like our life has purpose, but it is also our responsibility to work on trying to build this purpose. We need to reflect carefully on creating purpose and meaning — we don't just stumble across them. When I think of meaning-making, I often think of Viktor Frankl, the Jewish Austrian psychiatrist who developed logotherapy — a form of therapy based on searching for meaning as the primary motivational source. Frankl was sent to a concentration camp during World War II, and lost multiple family members to the gas chambers and illness. Despite these terrible experiences, he was able to find some meaning in his experiences, which helped him survive and support others. He wrote a bestselling book, *Man's Search for Meaning,* about these experiences and his framework.

Living according to a framework of meaning

Over time, I have found that my own framework of meaning involves being courageous, compassionate, and honest, shining light into areas of darkness and injustice, and being curious.

When living according to this framework, I find it easier to accept personal suffering, and to make choices aligned with this meaning. These choices can manifest in a range of ways. I have decided to mostly work in public mental health (versus the more lucrative private practice), to have a rescue greyhound (instead of buying a designer dog), and to speak up about unpopular issues, such as the importance of understanding the harm done to those in prison — despite the anger people may direct at me for these views. All these actions are values aligned, and were carefully considered decisions. I work in forensic public mental health because I believe in equity and access to healthcare for those who cannot afford private fees (and am especially passionate about care for those with complex needs, such as forensic clients). I chose to adopt a dog instead of buying one because I hold firm beliefs about the importance of rescuing instead of contributing to pet overpopulation, and the continued breeding of cute but incredibly unhealthy breeds such as pugs. I chose a greyhound because they come from terrible conditions within the cruel racing industry, a choice that aligns with my core value of compassion. A greyhound is an excellent fit for my inner-city lifestyle (another value — ensuring I provide good care when I take on a commitment or a dependent).

All this means that I am not overwhelmed by seeing harm in the world, as I feel I am taking some action against difficult things, not standing by helplessly and despairing. None of these actions will change the world, but they allow me to contribute to causes bigger than myself and give me a sense of purpose.

Of course, other people can hold the same values but choose to express them very differently. Many ways to find meaning come down to the individual. I know people who have found meaning in making art, raising children, writing, working in the fields of international aid, teaching, animal rescue, sport, and health, or in forming other close communities, but there are as many unique forms of meaning as there are people in the world. Tying meaning to our broader values instead of to certain goals or identities means we can hold onto the meaning even if we accomplish a goal, or if our identity shifts.

Finding your own meaning

It may be useful to spend some time considering what you think your meaning is.

* What makes you feel alive?
* What do you want to be remembered for when you die?
* What qualities do you admire in other people?
* How would you describe yourself in three words?
* If you could do anything to make things better (both for yourself, and others), what would it be?

And:

* What is one simple step you can take towards that action today?

These questions can help point you to a bigger framework that will support you during hard times.

When reflecting and working to build a good psychological framework with meaning for yourself, you may have to uproot some of your assumptions about life. 'Meaning' is bigger than common pursuits such as making money or having fun. These things are well and good, but the hedonic treadmill (more on that later!) means that we quickly adapt to new pleasurable activities and the happiness we feel returns to our usual level — so we have to keep chasing newer, bigger, and better ways of being happy. This is exhausting, resource-intensive, and won't provide long-term satisfaction. It's so important to find other ways of building a satisfying life.

Your values (and why they matter)

I commonly talk to clients about their values because values are fundamental to how we live. Values mean our standards of behaviour, or the things we think are important. They are not morals (a system of beliefs around good and bad) or ethics (reasoning how to do an action one thinks is good or right). There is some crossover, but values are usually internal (not imposed by society) and reveal those things we think are *truly* important. Life can be much messier than we think, and values are a great map for us as we try to rock-scramble around psychic chasms or abseil into abysses.

An incomplete list of common values:

- authenticity
- freedom
- compassion
- community
- connection
- adventure
- courage
- creativity
- determination
- perseverance
- love
- health
- honesty

Choosing how we spend our time and energy

No one can do or have it all. We each have innate capacities and skills, and we can develop and learn other skills as we go along with effort, training, and practice. The main difference between a fixed mindset — in which we believe that skill is innate — and a growth mindset — in which we believe that we can learn and develop skills with effort and practice — is that a growth mindset is more psychologically helpful: it allows us to view failure flexibly and to continue to develop new abilities over the course of our life.

Nevertheless, even if we consciously adopt a growth mindset, committing to a course of action (e.g., a hobby or a job) will have opportunity costs (the loss of the other alternatives when we make a choice) and use up time, energy, and money, thereby reducing the resources we have to do other things. We can try to stretch ourselves super thin to have it all or we can accept that we cannot and instead carefully select which opportunities we put our energy into.

We have infinite possibilities in this world, with finite time and resources, and need to find a way of choosing between options.

Why knowing our values matters

It helps us to choose how we spend our time

Values help us to identify opportunities that have meaning for us and to make wise decisions about our time. For example, holding the value of community might encourage us to prioritise social events where we can create lasting bonds (such as community gardening) rather than solo activities or those based only on having fun. (Everything in moderation, of course — fun is essential for life, too, as is solitude!)

Values help us to tolerate discomfort

Some types of therapy — like acceptance and commitment therapy (ACT) and humanistic therapy — also emphasise the importance of knowing your values, as knowing that you are moving towards them will help you tolerate some discomfort.

You are much more likely to be able to manage the pain of getting out of bed for a morning run on a cold winter morning, for example, if it links to a core value of health, than if you do it because you think you *should*, or to lose weight.

Values help us to understand ourselves and have a more resilient identity

Values are also useful to understand as part of our core identity. We can wed our identity entirely to aspects of our being, most often work roles or family relationships (e.g., Sally the psychologist, Tim the husband). However, this leaves our identity and sense of self-worth dependent on a single role. Losing this role, such as by retrenchment or divorce, can then result in a loss of identity and difficulties with mood. It is far better for long-term mental health to base our sense of identity on a range of values, and several role identities.

How to recognise and name your values

We can identify our own core values through reflecting, and by looking at what aspects or behaviours come up repeatedly in our lives (as one example, I read a lot and like learning — this points to a value of curiosity). Ideally, we want a small number of values, and the ability to hold them loosely and be *flexible*. Values are not just abstract ideas but are guiding principles we act on. If we have too many values to approach at the same time, we will feel confused and overstretched.

Values evolve as life progresses and that is okay, if we remain aware of this progression. Holding values loosely means recognising that sometimes reality will conflict with our values, and we might have to amend them, or may have to choose between two values — such as if we value both independence and community.

It can be tempting to be black and white about values.
Remember that they are guiding principles, instead of rules.

Some good questions to ask yourself when considering your values:

- What do I stand for?
- How do I show this in my daily life?
- Are my goals aligned with the values I have?
- How can you translate your values into action?
- What discomfort will I tolerate in the pursuit of these values?
- Which of my current actions are not values-aligned? And how can I tweak those actions to be more in line with my values?

Tweaking your expectations of yourself

A supportive structure for a life with meaning involves ensuring that we have realistic expectations of life. I was raised to believe that my life would be endlessly fulfilling, that happiness was the most important thing, that I could have and do anything if I worked for it, and that there would be constant progress and new goals.

As an adult, the expectations I had been taught didn't work. I found myself increasingly anxious and stressed about hitting my goals, swept up in never-ending lists of self-improvement measures (do yoga/meditate/go hiking/join a book club/read more work literature/go on a date a week/cook a new recipe a week/learn a sport), and was often distressed because I felt like I couldn't achieve the ideals (thin, beautiful, well groomed, happy, smart, busy, socially connected) being held up for me.

I suspect many of you hold similar unconscious beliefs and have had similar experiences.

> Happiness is just an emotion and not a goal — and certainly cannot be the end goal of life.
>
> To-do or to-experience lists grow endlessly, with new things added as soon as one thing gets ticked off.
>
> Fulfilment comes in fits and starts, most jobs have some grind, and there is no ultimate optimisation or finish line for life (beyond death).

Adjusting 'shoulds'

Most of these internalised expectations of ourselves and our lives can be framed as 'shoulds' — 'I should always strive for more.' 'I should do better each year.' Recognising this tendency in my own thinking and tweaking these 'shoulds' to make them more realistic has been transformative. I have learnt to accept some realistic truths in their place.

Replacing my shoulds with these concepts has given me more internal freedom and allowed me to more frequently find peace.

This shift has also translated to action (or conscious inaction), such as refusing to set new year's resolutions ('new year, new me' is one of the biggest lies we have ever been sold) and ensuring that I only add a new commitment to my to-do list once an existing one has been removed.

When you are trying to feel better, removing a few shoulds can be extremely helpful.

- Is there a should that is causing you pain?
- What can you replace it with?
- How can you avoid forming new shoulds?

Here are a few suggestions of practical steps you can take:

- Unsubscribe from ads from diet companies and other businesses that are trying to make you feel a certain way about yourself, or make you think you should be a certain way.
- Refuse to set yourself new year's resolutions or goals unless they are aligned with your core values.
- Practise a script for calmly but politely telling a family member that you are happy as you are and are not looking to lose weight/get married/change jobs.
- Before you buy something, ask yourself *a*. if you need it, *b*. if you can afford it, and *c*. whether it will *really* change your life (I always convince myself each new purchase will, and it never does).
- Unfollow social media accounts that promote unachievable aspirations.
- Stop setting yourself a new goal as soon as you achieve one. Instead, spend a few moments basking in the achievement and hard work you put in.

Many people fall into the fallacy of arrival (i.e., believing that when we make it, when we achieve something, we will finally be happy). I've been there myself, thinking that I'd be happy once I finished my doctorate, or found a partner, or bought a house, etc. We won't find contentment in the outcome, though, without contentment in the process.

Life is not perfect, and nor are you. You *will* feel pain and disappointment, you *will* make mistakes and sometimes fail. If you can accept these things as being intrinsically part of a 'good' life, you are far more likely to be mentally healthy than if you work too hard at pushing them away.

FURTHER READING

The Happiness Trap — Russ Harris

A book by a proponent of acceptance and commitment therapy (ACT) focused on helping us learn to explore and tolerate difficult emotions and experiences, and supporting us to move away from chasing happiness.

Finding your tribe

Each time I see T-shirts or art prints saying 'your vibe attracts your tribe', I cringe. Yet, it's somewhat true. NOT in a weird, hippy 'energetic attraction' way (I don't hold much stock in that stuff), but because we know that people tend to cluster with others who are most like them, and we are strongly influenced by those closest to us.

I dislike the common idea that we should curate our social circles to help us achieve certain goals — this feels mechanical, transactional, and hollow. We can't be truly close to people if we're focused on how we can use them to better ourselves. It is, however, important to make sure we have people we can be vulnerable with, and that these people support us with our journey and goals, even if they are on different pathways.

We need to feel connected, and we need a tribe, or a few tribes. Our brains are wired for close connection and belonging, and lack of connection can contribute to mental health issues, including anxiety and depression.

The focus in contemporary society is often on finding a partner, which ignores the other connections we can build. While having a partner can be positive for our wellbeing, one person alone can *never* meet our needs. We need larger groups and to feel embedded in a community, not just in a single relationship. This focus on partnering up instead of building community is, in part, driving the high rates of isolation and loneliness I encounter in my work.

When I was struggling with mental health in my early twenties, many things helped, including good therapy and medication. One of the most important things I did, though, was to address my sense of social isolation: the feeling that no one would like me, that I couldn't make friends and would never be loved. This message came from a few places: my family, social anxiety, teasing and rejection at school, and troubling romantic relationships. It kept me stuck alone, wanting to be part of 'normal life' but not knowing how.

Strategies for building your tribe

Busting this self-myth that I couldn't make friends and would never be loved took a few things. Most important was recognising that it *was* a myth and starting to broaden my circles and approach people to extend invitations. I still do this, and in an even more blatant and unashamed way now, often sidling up to people I have met and liked and saying, 'Will you be my friend?' Try it, it works (the trick is to be humorous and self-deprecating, so people don't think you are a total creep; and to recognise and respect when people don't want to be your friend). It's also important to be aware of gender and power dynamics, and to ensure that you don't have ulterior motives or come across as intrusive or sleazy. Other things that helped included throwing myself into things I liked doing, contributing to other people's lives, and learning to be more settled in my own.

Knowing how to find your tribe is hard, I know. There is no easy fix, and it can take a while as you play with and try out different identities and groups. Overall, we are more likely to find good friends and connections where we spend the most time, where people are most like us, and in closest geographical proximity to us (though the internet has changed this). This is why spaces like work, study, and regular hobbies, like a choir or weekly games night, are so important.

Enter the real world

Remote work might make finding a tribe a little harder, so keeping a balance between staying home and being out in the world is vital in forming new connections. I should note that online interactions can be a start to finding in-real-life friends (IRL, as we used to say back in the day) but are not a full replacement for face-to-face connections. Online spaces can become polarised echo chambers, and we lose richness and variety in interaction when we *only* exist in those spaces. Working out how to move online connections to face-to-face ones (at least sometimes) is vital for wellbeing, though I acknowledge that for some this will feel difficult. Even if meeting in person is impossible, moving from texting to video is a great start towards deeper connection.

Find people who share your values

Living a values-aligned life is likely to mean we enter spaces where we find people like us. I often find friends in places like book groups, writing groups, and greyhound-parent circles, where people share my interests and values. Other people I know have made friends from community theatre, volunteering, sport, skydiving, and martial arts.

Having a good tribe means knowing what you want from your connections with other people. Sometimes we fall into connections based on proximity without stopping to think about what we truly value in other people. This relies on first knowing our own values. I have a small handful of people who are closest to me (research shows we cannot maintain more than a small number — approximately five — very close connections) and a larger number of friends and friendly acquaintances.

We need people in our lives at all these levels of intimacy.

If you stop and think about the people you are closest to, what do you like about them, and where did you meet them? What do you value in people? What do you want to avoid? How do you show up for others?

It is also important to think about who you want to be in your relationships. This is just as essential as what you want. What do you have to offer? What do you bring your tribe? How do you support those you love?

Work on being the best friend/colleague/peer/partner you can be.

If you realise that you tend to find your closest people in certain settings (such as the library), what can you do to increase the likelihood you will meet new people there? Can you start a book club? Attend a hobby-specific meet-up group?

Tolerate discomfort and false starts

We might have to learn to tolerate the discomfort of putting ourselves out there, or trying to meet new people with no success. Sometimes, focusing on the process and the skills we are learning is most important, even if the outcome isn't quite what we want. Building enduring and lasting connections can take time and have many false starts. This is part of life.

Examine beliefs and actions that may be blocking you

Sometimes we hold internalised beliefs, such as feeling unlikeable or unworthy, or believing that other people can't be trusted, that become obstacles to finding our tribe. We may feel at war with ourselves, wanting to belong but also pushing against it. We might want friends but never actually show up to things or invite other people out. Perhaps we take, and don't give. Maybe our expectations are unrealistic. We might have issues with social or communication skills, or struggle with rejection. All these things can be addressed.

Social anxiety and focusing on what other people think of us is a common stumbling block. The most potent cure I have found for social anxiety involves realising how little headspace other people give us — most people are focused on worrying about what other people think of *them*, not about what they think of you.

Finding our tribe means accepting that we need tribe members. We need to be willing to reflect on who our tribe may be, what we want from them, what we bring to them, how we show up, and what discomforts we are prepared to tolerate in the pursuit of connection and belonging.

Your inner wilds: exploring feelings and thoughts

Understanding our inner experiences is vital for psychological well-being. Our thoughts, feelings, and behaviours are connected, and how we perceive and think about things can make the proverbial 'heaven out of hell, or hell out of heaven'.

In this section, we'll explore key concepts about emotion and thought, learn to manage difficult feelings, and explore ways to manage how − and what − we think. We'll also bust some emotional-management myths, and learn why avoidance of difficult emotion is so problematic, as well as how to approach emotion with wisdom and self-compassion.

What are emotions?

Emotions are a wonderful sense we can use to navigate the world; the true sixth sense. An emotion is a feeling that arises from either your internal processes, your relationship with others, or the situation you are in — or a combination of all these things. They have developed, from an evolutionary perspective, to give us *information*.

Some examples include:

- anger
- sadness
- fear
- disgust
- love
- shock
- joy
- shame
- happiness
- guilt
- loneliness
- boredom
- anxiety

- resentment
- fury
- envy
- satisfaction
- pride
- embarrassment
- hatred
- jealousy
- helplessness
- disgruntlement
- overwhelm
- panic
- anticipation

Emotions get a bad rap at times, and are often described as overblown, scary, or difficult to manage. Most people (including me!) have a range of behaviours aimed at avoiding some feelings (eating, intoxication, social-media and phone use, sex, detachment) and others aimed at chasing feelings (buying new things, planning new experiences compulsively, or trying to force positivity). Difficulties managing feelings brings three-quarters of my clients into my therapy room, and at its core is often severe discomfort when difficult emotions come up.

Why do we have emotions?

All emotions help us stay alive. Disgust can help us notice that something is rotten and/or likely to make us unwell; love can help us pair bond, thus ensuring the continuity of the species. As our world has increased in complexity, emotions too have morphed, generalised, and taken on new functions and meanings. Our anxiety and fear (evolutionarily intended to alert us to danger to keep us alive) is no longer caused by the sighting of a sabre-toothed tiger; instead, we fear more formless and longer-lasting threats, such as a performance review or public speaking. This makes those fears harder to manage, as we can't use our usual fight/flight responses, and must instead engage higher-order processes, such as reframing thoughts or practising mindfulness strategies. We need to learn these skills; they aren't innate.

Over the course of a good life, we will feel all kinds of emotions every day. Emotions will fluctuate, and learning to be okay with these changes and with tolerating and navigating emotional states is vital. We will never be able to engage in activities that matter if we hide at the first sign of distress. When we try to run away from emotions (called 'experiential avoidance'), we usually find that we'll also start to avoid more activities and limit what we do, and we'll end up with harder emotions to manage.

Emotions are never problematic in and of themselves. They each have their use, and we all have our own emotional 'map', based on our temperaments and which emotions were encouraged in our families.

But our emotions don't always reflect reality, just as our thoughts are not always truth. It's helpful to learn to recognise and tend to our emotions, but also to hold them at a distance at times, and examine them objectively as information.

Learning your emotional map

It can be helpful to learn your emotional map, and the function each emotion has for you — why it comes up in certain situations and what it is communicating. For instance, your feeling of sadness might be encouraging you to stay cocooned at home, giving you the quiet time you need to process a loss. It may also be communicating to other people that you need support. Scientists have found that tears based on emotion have a higher protein content than reflex tears, which happen if you get something in your eye. Emotional tears are more viscous and drip down our face more slowly, perhaps increasing the likelihood that other people will notice. Our bodies are smart!

Similarly, anger might be protecting you and may also act as a signal to people to give you space. By learning to understand what our emotions are trying to communicate to us, as well as when they might be brought up, we can get better at the work of observing them objectively and taking their cues.

There are two arms to emotional management. First, learning to name and make space for all emotions and using them as information. Second, developing some skills to soothe really difficult emotions (often called 'distress tolerance'). We'll explore both of these in this chapter and the next.

The first step: know and name your emotions

Emotions can become problematic due to how you *express them* (i.e., being angry is okay, hitting someone is not), when they are too *intense*, or when they *change too frequently* and cause you difficulties and distress.

Emotional management is the process of learning to name, understand, and respond to feelings. Big feelings are okay — and to be expected when handling difficult subjects like climate change, or personal or global tragedies — but it's important to know what to do with them.

The first step to managing emotions is to *name them as they arise*. Naming an emotion gives it shape, so our brain can recognise it, often reducing our distress. Trying to understand what an emotion might be telling us and what triggered it is helpful for building emotional awareness. Being able to say to yourself 'I felt sad when X didn't say hello to me, and it made me worry about whether people like me or not, because I have a history of feeling isolated' can be helpful.

Learning to name emotions can be hard at the start. Simple meditation practices like a guided body scan are helpful for learning to notice the emotions we feel, as most emotions have distinct bodily signs and we can learn to identify them by noticing where we feel them in our body. Anxiety usually brings tightness in our chest and shoulders, while sadness can feel like a weight through the body. Something physical, like yoga, can also be helpful, as it slows our minds and helps us tune into our emotional state and body.

Accept difficult emotions in advance

Accepting in advance as best we can that we will inevitably feel pain, including sadness, anger, fear, hurt, grief, loss, and loneliness is essential. We will die, and before we die, we will likely experience physical pain. We will age and our bodies will change. We will lose people we love. Relationships will end. We will be forced to sit alone with ourselves. Accepting all of this means that when we experience an emotion, we won't panic and throw ourselves into a search for a quick way to fix it, but we will instead explore it and place it in context.

It's important to regularly practise the emotional skills of naming and accepting as we begin to build emotional management, and meditation certainly helps. We don't need to devote hours to it: even a simple ten-minute yoga practice and five minutes of breath meditation is an excellent start. Keeping our goals simple and achievable is much better than aiming too high.

Befriend emotions when they arise

Managing emotion requires accepting that emotions are a natural response to life and to specific sociocultural settings. It's *not* a mental health problem if something painful occurs (such as a school shooting) and you experience intense distress — this is a realistic and normal response to an awful situation. Good emotional management means accepting a feeling (although not the event, necessarily), learning to breathe into it and make space for it, and learning to befriend it.

While the concept of 'befriending' an emotion may seem odd, it follows on from recognising that all emotions are useful. I notice that when I travel alone, I feel very lonely as I acclimatise to being away from my usual busy social and work life. However, solitude and slowing down is a huge part of the joy of solo travel, and over time I've learnt to tolerate and accept my loneliness, realise that it's just part of adjustment to a slower pace, and even see it as something poignant and beautiful to experience.

An interesting exercise to try is to invite an emotion to sit down beside you and to talk to it. This requires some imagination, of course, but it can be a way to become familiar with each emotion, including what purpose it serves for you. Some questions to ask it might be:

- Why are you here?
- What are you trying to tell me?
- Am I listening to you?
- What do you need from me?

Visualisation and imagery techniques are helpful here, as 'making space' for emotion is a vague concept, I know. I use a technique derived from ACT, where I close my eyes and visualise the feeling getting bigger, noticing what it looks like, its colour, how heavy it is, where it goes in my body. This allows me to really lean into the emotion, and then to befriend it — and I often find that as I do this, it becomes more manageable and less scary.

Over time, we want to build a good set of daily 'emotional hygiene' practices, so we can experience, understand, and process emotions as they arise. I provide some examples of daily emotional management skills below, and in the next chapter we'll explore ways to manage really hard emotions.

Practices for everyday emotional management:

- Care for your physical needs, including sleep, ensure you manage any symptoms of illness and attend to your body, feed yourself well, and move your body.
- Have an honest chat with a supportive friend, or a therapy session. It's important to use these spaces not just to vent but also to engage in constructive exploration and problem-solving (where applicable).
- Regularly engage in sensory activities, such as cooking a meal, playing or listening to music, spending time in nature, or gardening. Immersing yourself in sensory activity increases mindfulness and pleasure.
- Some form of regular check-in with yourself. An example might be starting your day by taking your emotional temperature, and asking yourself what you need. Journaling regularly to explore and process your thoughts or feelings can also be helpful. For those who don't like writing, expressive art can serve a similar function.
- Building a vocabulary of compassionate self-talk (e.g., 'this too will pass') and learning to question your thinking ('when was the last time something really bad happened?', 'how likely is it that the worst case will happen?').

Managing pointy feels

When we experience really difficult emotions that are threatening to take over (e.g., having a panic attack, wanting to self-harm, or responding with aggression), it can be helpful to have a specific subset of skills we can draw on to help us navigate these hard times. In this chapter, we'll explore some of these skills. You should use these skills only when emotions are most pointy, and at other times continue with the other emotional management practices we've already discussed above. This is important because we need to learn to tolerate and accept emotion instead of rushing to reduce it or block it.

When we try to block emotion, it's often because we feel a frantic sense of 'this emotion needs to go away, I can't stand it', and may find that we move from activity to activity in a rushed bid to repress. Soothing, on the other hand, means acknowledging the emotion ('I feel this, and it's okay, it will pass over time, I just need to get through it') and gentle, planned emotional-regulation activities.

Bodily techniques to process emotions

Incorporating bodily techniques into emotional management can be a potent way of soothing pointy emotions.
Sadness, for instance, might need some time in bed and
a weighted blanket, while anger might mean a pavement-
pounding run with some loud music to burn off adrenaline,
some expressive art or writing, or an energetic dance to
some loud music, and anxiety might need paced breathing
and a calming yoga stretch.

Exercise can release endorphins and serve as a great
distractor and way to blow off steam. You could take a
walk with your dog, or spend some time outdoors. Being
in nature, whether a forest, on top of a mountain, or a
wide-open space, has been shown to have many benefits
for mental health, helping to soothe sadness, angst, anxiety,
and anger.

Share our emotions in constructive ways

Expressing and sharing feelings can also lessen their impact
(though unconstructive venting does not help, and has been
shown to actually impede emotional management). The
difference between sharing and venting can be subtle, and
is found in whether we are seeking succour, care, and to
be soothed, or are primarily looking for someone to agree
with us. The crux of learning to manage pointy emotions
involves finding ways to soothe them that are not simple
avoidance ('I just won't think about that'), or mindless self-
soothing (such as through screen use or alcohol).

Ride the wave (this too will pass)

Emotions will come and go; learning to ride them like a wave can be helpful when they are flooding you. Emotions occur on a spectrum of intensity, and even the most difficult ones will typically peak in 30 minutes and will then begin to recede.

Distress tolerance can sometimes involve tolerating pain until it starts to shift a little.

I often teach people how to 'ride the wave' of emotions. It's helpful to ask yourself to recall the last time you felt bad, and then ask yourself if it lasted forever. When we feel bad, it is almost always made worse by fear that things will stay the same, but no matter how hard the feeling is, it will pass.

Bodily and somatic soothing techniques

Bodily or somatic techniques can help manage explosive distress. Using cold to counteract the heat of emotion reduces physiological activation. A blast of cold water or an icepack on one's forehead can work wonders. Immersing your face in cold water can trigger the mammalian dive reflex (a biological response) and reduce heart rate (therefore reducing the physical symptoms of anxiety). If cold immersion doesn't appeal, a hot shower can also be very soothing!

Other aids include lavender oil, weighted blankets or pillows, sensory fiddle toys, calming music, and warmth. All of these aids evoke comfort, can reduce external stimulation, and can influence polyvagal output. The polyvagal system is the bodily system responsible for regulating physiological activation, and it connects with our central nervous system, helping us 'hack' our emotions by influencing our body.

Breathe for the polyvagal system

Managing the polyvagal system helps soothe distress. When we are heightened, the quickest way to influence this is through our breath.

Breathing slowly, with a focus on a longer exhale than inhale is key to activating the polyvagal system, and I often work with clients on practising 4 (inhale), 2 (hold), 6 (exhale) breathing. Another useful exercise is 'box breathing', where we inhale to the count of 4, hold for 4, and exhale for 4. This calms us physically, and gives our brain something to focus on, thus acting as a circuit breaker.

Meditate

Some specific meditation techniques, like 'leaves on a stream' (where you watch each thought and let it go, just as leaves float down a stream) that are drawn from ACT can also be helpful as they help us build our capacity to observe thoughts and feelings, without getting too swept up.

Occupy the brain

Engaging in intellectual or creative activities, such as pottery, painting, crosswords, or playing with your make-up collection. No right or wrongs here, just whatever you enjoy. Occupying the brain can reduce rumination as the brain processes cognitive stress (which we tend to prefer to emotional stress).

Evoke the opposite emotion

Another helpful technique involves deliberately evoking an opposite emotion — an excellent skill drawn from dialectical behaviour therapy (DBT) — because the body and brain cannot perceive two emotions at once. This can be powerful when used strategically — by watching some slapstick comedy (*Fawlty Towers* is my favourite, don't judge me) when very sad, or doing something loving when resentment or envy surface.

Learn to STOP

Another useful DBT skill is called 'STOP'. This stands for Stopping (freezing and pausing all action as you name the emotion), Taking a step back to evaluate the situation, Observing what you are feeling and thinking to gather relevant facts, and Proceeding mindfully, by asking yourself questions like 'what do I want from this situation?' or, 'what am I hoping to achieve?'

Learning consequential thinking (i.e., if I do this, then this will happen) is a great skill for overpowering emotions like anger.

Plan ahead: prepare a self-soothing toolkit

If you often struggle with certain strong emotions, it's a good idea to spend some time preparing a physical and mental toolkit of things you can use to soothe yourself. This is a common strategy used in DBT, where people use toolkits to help them cope with overwhelmingly difficult emotions (such as fear, anger, shame, or grief).

We can also plan ahead for difficult times. It's useful to notice when an emotionally difficult situation is about to arise (e.g., a visit with a problematic family member) and plan ahead for how we will cope with it, including soothing activities before the event, plans for the actual event (Do we need time limits? A friend on call?) and ways to decompress after the event. Planning our emotional lives in this manner means that we can experience difficult situations and emotions with a sense of safety.

Objects to add to a self-soothing toolkit might include:

- some beautiful and affirming quotes on cards
- chamomile tea
- a weighted toy
- a scented candle
- sensory toys
- a book you love
- favourite podcasts
- a meditation video
- a favourite yoga practice
- white-noise sounds
- essential oils
- a puzzle
- craft supplies

- a bar of chocolate (don't knock it, comfort eating is also a tool)

Your mental toolkit might include:

- the phone numbers of friends you can call for support, advice, and guidance
- a reminder that hard times will pass
- some meditation practices
- a favourite cafe or place you can go to feel connected to people without pressure
- a reminder to walk away and give yourself space
- a gentle and self-compassionate inner voice
- a list of things you do well or are proud of
- a voice memo from your psychologist reminding you that you are okay
- a post-it note with a reminder to stop and think before acting
- an inspiring and kind note from a friend — or yourself!

Thoughts (are not always truth)

All human beings are born with a special ability, and a part of the brain that sets us apart from all other animals. This part of the brain is the prefrontal cortex and it's very well developed in humans, conferring on us the ability to engage in complex thought processes, including thinking about the past and future, planning, organising, and making tricky decisions by performing cost-benefit analysis and comparing different options.

These skills are a blessing, because they have brought us to the technological point where I can sit on my couch, turn a computer on, connect with strangers in other countries, control my lighting from an app on my phone, and shout at Alexa to turn on my timer. Conversely, these same abilities can also keep me awake at night worrying about whether my holiday will get cancelled due to floods, trap me in paralysis because I cannot choose between two options, and lock me into anxiety because I can't stop dwelling on the thought that my backache is actually a tumour in my spine.

Thoughts influence how we feel and what we do, and thus they influence our reality. There is nothing mystical about this — we change our behaviours in response to our thoughts, and our behaviours have consequences.

We all think, *all the time*, but we don't often pause to think about *what* we think about, why we think, when we think or how much we think. Understanding patterns of healthy thinking and maintaining a meta-cognitive awareness (thinking about what we think) of our thought processes is one of the keys to managing our mental health. Thoughts are not reality, nor are they objective truth — they are just learnt neural patterns based on repetition. We have thousands of thoughts daily, and some difficult and painful thoughts are just learnt habits we repeat unknowingly. As with emotions, learning to notice, understand, and use thoughts well is essential.

Most mental health difficulties come with trouble with *what we think* (negative thoughts about ourselves and the world, or anxious thoughts), *how we think* (rumination, obsessional patterns), and *how much we believe* what we think. Good functioning involves some measure of control over our brains and thinking processes by building patterns of realistic and helpful thought.

Thoughts don't arise in a vacuum. When a baby is born, the brain is a relatively clean slate, and a baby will operate from instinct and the basic drives (warmth, food, comfort). As a baby grows and its brain develops, it will start to develop language and with this, thoughts. It is important to remember that thinking is a habit, and that we often develop sets of thoughts that we default to at difficult times (for example, one of mine used to be around the idea of 'failure' if I was unable to grasp something or learn a skill). We develop habitual and biased thought patterns based on influences from our family (especially our primary caregivers) and the broader culture around us, including extended families, schools, peer groups, teachers, and media influences. We like to believe that we have free will, but the reality is that we are shaped significantly by those around us.

The relationship between thoughts and feelings (and therefore wellbeing) has been much studied. One area of study is cognitive behavioural therapy (CBT), a therapy focused on helping us understand the links between our thoughts, feelings, and behaviours, and making changes in how these operate to reduce symptoms of mental health distress. Research on CBT shows that working on making our thinking more realistic and helpful can lead to changes in how we feel and thus our behaviours. Thoughts and emotions work together. We think a certain way, often because of how we were raised and what we were taught. For example, if we were repeatedly told that 'the world is dangerous and bad things will happen', we may have experienced emotions, like anxiety, that caused us to change our behaviours (and resulted in us becoming avoidant). Over time, these loops can strengthen, sometimes resulting in diagnosable mental illnesses.

Noticing these loops is a helpful skill to have when things go wrong (when something difficult happens and we experience distressing emotions) but also just for daily life, because so much of what we choose to do is based on how we think about situations.

Of course, CBT is not a panacea for all ills, and sometimes difficulties *are* external (such as a bad boss, or an abusive partner) and are better changed in the real world than reframed in our heads. CBT (and therapy in general) should never be used to help us accept poor treatment.

Manage what we think
Recognise thought patterns

An example. Reflect upon a time you were rejected from something that was important to you — a job, a relationship, anything. There are a range of thoughts you can have about this situation. I have listed two sets here. Each will give rise to different feelings and change how you act.

> Thought # 1: *Of course I was rejected. I knew I was not good enough and should not have even tried. I am never going to get what I want and should just stop trying.*

> Thought # 2: *Well, that sucks and I am sad, but I understand that rejection happens. Everyone has experienced rejection at some stage in life. I wonder if I can learn something from this?*

How would you feel after both these thoughts? How would they influence your behaviour? Learning to notice *what* you think is crucial, but it's common to miss this and go straight from external event/trigger to emotion.

We fall into habitual patterns of thinking — such as those people who experience anxiety and catastrophise instinctively without knowing they are doing so. These habitual ways of thinking colour all we do and feel.

Some habitual and problematic ways of thinking involve:

- expecting the worst (catastrophising; 'I know I will be fired today')
- filtering out the positive and focusing on the negative

- black and white thinking (forgetting to view alternatives: 'there is nothing good about her at all')
- reasoning based only on emotion ('I feel anxious about this so it must be dangerous')
- reading people's minds ('I am certain they don't like me')
- predicting the future ('I know this won't go well')
- jumping to conclusions ('He didn't say hello to me, he must be mad at me')
- generalising from one instance to the global (e.g., 'Sarah doesn't like me, this means no one likes me').

Most of these patterns skew to the negative, because our brains look for danger and hook into fear as a means of keeping us safe. Evolutionarily, it was more adaptive for us to look for the snakes than notice the rainbows — because the snakes could kill us — and we've carried these tendencies through to the modern day. We lose perspective at difficult times, and can amplify difficulties, or catastrophise.

Create space around thoughts and evaluate them

Good management of thinking means noticing habitual thought patterns, learning to recognise and create space around them, and slowly replacing them. Creating space around a thought by saying something like 'I am having the thought that ...' allows us to separate from it a little, and recognise it as a thought instead of as objective reality. Essentially, we want to become our own therapists and reality-testers by being able to tease apart our thoughts, drill down into them, and decide if we keep or discard them.

Learning to examine our own thinking involves asking

ourselves a range of questions to evaluate our thinking. Questions I encourage clients to ask themselves include:

- What is the evidence for and against this thought?
- Is this thinking just a habit?
- In what ways is this thought untrue?
- Are there important pieces of the puzzle I am missing?
- Is this thought helpful or realistic?
- Are there alternative ways I could think about this?
- What would someone else (such as a close friend) say about this?
- What would I say to someone else (such as a close friend) who told me they were thinking this way?

We all tend to seek confirming evidence for our way of seeing the world and ignore what is contradictory to our thoughts and beliefs. I thought of myself as a quitter for a long time, because of some childhood experiences where I tried and failed to commit to hobbies. Once I sat down and made a list of all the things I *had* stuck out, I realised how untrue this was. I also worked out that quitting things I wasn't enjoying was fine (see ya later, aerial hoop classes). This exercise will force you to stop and examine the validity of your thoughts, and look at the bigger picture outside the microscopic view of your habitual way of thinking.

We want telescopes, not microscopes.

Replace thoughts with more realistic ones

The final step in managing what we think is to determine what a more realistic thought might be. For instance, working with the thought 'I will never find love' might lead us to the more realistic thought 'I may or may not have another intimate relationship, but I notice that I have love in my life in a range of ways at present.'

If you find that some of your worries are driven by thoughts that are unhelpful or untrue, it is good to think of how you can reframe them.

Is there a softer or more compassionate voice to use?

Can you be less certain about a bad outcome?

Can you look at evidence that disproves what you think?

Manage how much we think

Sometimes it is not the content of the thought that is a problem, but the fact that thoughts occur frequently, stick around for a long time, return over and over, and occur at rapid-fire pace, all of which can make them seem uncontrollable. Rumination (going over the same thought repeatedly) is a feature of many mental illnesses, including anxiety and depression. While it may be helpful to challenge the *content* of any ruminative thought, it can also be beneficial to work on managing this style of thinking. Rumination can take away much of our capacity to be present, to engage with what is, and to find enjoyment or focus.

Tips for managing rumination

Train your attention

Rumination occurs when we have limited control over our brains and thoughts control us. Meditation and mindfulness practices can be very helpful. Creating a specific space and time where we sit down and deliberately focus on being present and watching our thoughts is a great way to start to build some attention. Eventually, we can expand this practice and bring it into other facets of life (e.g., focused time on a writing project, mindful gardening). I love Tara Brach's meditations, and for shorter pops of calm will use an app such as Smiling Mind or Headspace, or just the mindfulness timer on my watch.

Minimise multitasking

There are times when we have to multitask, but we can also learn to pay full attention to an activity. This gently trains our brain and reduces chatter. We will need to exercise this skill daily, especially in our information-heavy world! While we think multitasking makes us more efficient, our brain cannot actually focus on two things at once, so each time we switch from one task to the other, we use valuable cognitive resources and end up being less efficient overall.

Conscious distraction

Distraction is helpful sometimes, but it cannot be the only tool in our toolbox. We must use it sparingly, saving it for times when we are very distressed or can't manage our thoughts and emotions in any other way. It's best to pick a distraction activity that matches what is occurring and how we are feeling. For instance, if we are feeling low and having sad thoughts, staying in bed and deliberately watching an episode of our favourite, funny TV show might be helpful. If we are very angry, then going for a run is more likely to be helpful because we will have energy to burn and can't ruminate as much when pushing our body.

Worry time

If we find that we are worrying a lot, it's helpful to set aside some time each day to worry and to engage in some problem-solving. I would recommend half an hour at a time, not too close to bedtime. Spend this focused time worrying, write the worries down, write some solutions down, and then put the worries aside until the same time tomorrow.

Write down worries

This is somewhat related to the above and is especially applicable for those who tend to ruminate at night, in a way that impacts sleep. This is very common, and it's problematic because we usually can't do anything about the things we worry about in the middle of the night, when everyone else is asleep. Instead of lying in bed and ruminating, it's much more useful to write down the worries with the idea that we will pick them up in the morning when we have the capacity to do something about them.

Reflect

Spend some time reflecting on whether worrying is helpful, and consider broadening your perspective. We often worry because we feel it serves a purpose, or keeps us safe. If we spend time identifying the worst things that could happen and planning for them, surely that will mean we're equipped to manage any difficulties that may arise, yes? Unfortunately not. Worry brings an illusory sense of safety, at a sometimes-high cost. Some questions to ask yourself:

- When has the worst case ever happened?
- Does my worry help resolve things?
- If the thing I am fearing did happen, would I cope?

The answer to the last question is almost always yes: we are good at underestimating our own resilience and capacity to adapt.

FURTHER READING

Changing Your Thinking – Sarah Edelman
A book about the basic principles of cognitive behavioural therapy, focused on supporting you to understand the patterns in your thinking, linking these to psychological difficulties, and learning to amend unhelpful patterns.

Radical acceptance

We often respond to difficult emotions and experiences by trying to push away and avoid. Over time, this leads us into all kinds of difficulties, as we do more and more to avoid emotions or experiences, which can eventually shut down normal processing and narrow our engagement with the world.

We'll all have times when life seems intolerable, when emotions are strong or flat, when we or other people make a mistake, or when difficult things happen. For a good, mentally healthy life, we need to accept that sometimes, we'll fall over, and we need to be able to climb (or grudgingly haul) ourselves back up.

Radical acceptance is a way to experience the world, where we approach and move *through* difficult things, instead of trying to move *around* them. In the next section, I'll explain why this is important, and how it can help us.

So, what is radical acceptance?

It's a concept plucked from DBT — and deeper — from the annals of Buddhism, and it's an essential part of living well with meaning.

When I first introduce the concept to clients, it often rankles, because they think that it means that we *approve* of everything — even difficult, traumatic, or unfair things.

Acceptance is different from approval, and radical acceptance means that we accept and understand that life will always contain difficulties, whether physical or emotional — and that a good and meaningful life means we accept these (even if we also work to change them where possible), instead of pretending them away. There are difficulties common to every society and life, such as death, illness, emotional pain, and physical pain — we cannot avoid these. Accepting them can free us up to have painful conversations and notice hard things. We can't change other people's behaviours, or the past, and radical acceptance means there's less chance of getting stuck in anger and indignation, hopefully shifting us towards helpful problem-solving instead.

When we accept difficulties, our pain becomes more tolerable as we compassionately and honestly address it, instead of defending against it. Asking questions such as *why me* can sometimes just move us further into guilt and shame — if there *is* a true 'why', maybe it's that we have in some way been defective or brought misfortune on ourselves. Acceptance can also free us up to try more things, as we accept that we will sometimes experience difficulties, such as anxiety when attempting something new.

Before I started practising radical acceptance, I was anxious about many things: failing, being disliked, or seeming silly. Radically accepting that I will sometimes say silly things, be disliked, or not quite get it right has changed my life and has given me freedom to try many things (hiking! pottery! skating!), which has made my life a lot more meaningful and FUN (even if I do always complain vociferously about uphill hikes).

Radical acceptance is *not* surrender or approval. It doesn't involve turning a blind eye to suffering or injustice because 'it is what it is'. It's instead turning *towards* the suffering and saying, 'I see you; I see what's happening, this is painful, what is happening is difficult.' It gives us the power to face difficulties, as we can recognise what is unfair/unkind/painful and work to change those things.

Acceptance of self

There is no radical acceptance without an acceptance of self. This includes acceptance of your physical self — your age, weight, shape, size, looks, and abilities, as well as your emotional and psychological self, with all its frailties and failings. Often you will struggle with one of these aspects more than the others.

Acceptance of your physical self

Many people struggle with accepting their physical shape and size, or how they look. Society has long placed huge value on our appearance, and on youth. Of course, how we look is no measure of our inner attributes or contentment, and many entirely average-looking people live very fulfilling lives. Age can bring immense benefits, including wisdom, knowledge, and a focus on what truly matters, even as we move away from youthful attractiveness (and really, the only alternative to ageing is death).

We can't reject fundamental parts of ourselves, such as our bodies — or the process of ageing — without rejecting who we are. Tackling diet culture and the entire weight-loss, anti-ageing, and beauty industry is a little outside the scope of this book (I could write a whole book on it alone!), but if this is something you struggle with, I urge you to look up some body-neutrality or body-positivity resources, investigate the Health at Every Size and the Intuitive Eating movements, and seek therapy if you have significant difficulties in this area.

When I struggle with my own body image, I ask myself a few questions to help myself assess and shift some of my body anxiety. These might be useful questions to ask yourself, too.

- Will anyone else notice this thing (pimple, stray chin hair, bit of fat) as much as I do?
- Does my feeling bad about myself benefit someone else? (The answer is usually the beauty, wellness, and diet industries.)
- Does this thing I despair over affect how my body functions?
- Is it central to who I am?
- Does it change who I am as a person?
- Do I notice when my friends gain weight/have a pimple? Do I judge them for it? (We often treat our friends with much more kindness than we treat ourselves.)
- Is looking good my job?

It can be helpful to take your attention off the small imperfections you obsess over (i.e., stop looking in the mirror or checking your body), remember that your job is not to look pretty, and that you have a wider and more glorious life than physical appearance alone. Values-based living (as discussed in earlier chapters) helps here. When you feel bad about your physical self, try to remember your values and the ways you find meaning. Not only will it become obvious how little your physical appearance has to do with living towards those values, but you will likely become refocused on something that *does* uphold those values and find yourself able to forget that pimple on your chin.

It's important to remember a few things about body image. Humans are very bad at estimating physical sizes. If we hyper-focus on certain parts of our bodies we start to see them out of proportion and not in the context of a whole moving body. Constantly checking (by weighing ourselves or checking the tightness of our jeans, for example) just reinforces these difficulties.

Body acceptance is so important. If we are focused on hating our bodies and reducing their size, we will have no time or energy for the bigger things that truly matter. I like to remind myself that who I am in this moment and how I spend *this* moment makes up the sum of my days. I don't want to be 80, thinking about how I spent my precious *few* years on earth agonising over my belly bulge.

Bodies shrink and grow, they bloat, spread, expand, meander, slip, sag, bleed, leak, sprout. They also do incredible things for us daily. Breath is a complex wonder, as are the heartbeat and thought. Learning more about the science of my body gives me more respect for it, and I focus less on how it looks and more on how much it does to keep me alive.

To radically accept your body, try to:

- Focus on the function of your body, not how it looks. Notice how much it does for you to keep you alive. Thank your body. Sometimes a simple exercise like placing your hand on each body part and thanking it can feel wonderful (if a little silly initially!) — this is especially useful for those parts of your body you struggle with. Sometimes using your body for enjoyment or pleasure can increase acceptance as you see what it does. Can you go on a hike? Hula hoop? Have an orgasm?
- Focus on body neutrality, not positivity. You don't have to love your body and think it looks fantastic, but you do need to cherish it and care for it because of the wonderful things it lets you experience and do.
- Focus on the things you like about your body. Do you like your softness? Strength? Skin? Nails? The silkiness of your hair? Notice and focus on these parts.
- Self-compassion meditation practices can be especially helpful when having a bad body image day. Focus on bringing compassion to the sadness and shame, and you will find that your relationship with your body softens.
- Care for your body well regardless of how you think it looks. It still deserves nutrition, hydration, to be cleaned and moisturised, to be stretched and moved, and to feel healthy and feel good. Take care to do all these things on bad body days. Something as simple as using a favourite moisturiser can start to shift things.
- Find clothes that feel comfortable and look good/fit you well (please throw out or donate those old jeans you can't

fit into!). Keeping clothes around in the hope that you will lose weight is like popping an opened can of tuna under your bed — a constant, unpleasant reminder.

Acceptance of your emotional self

Radical acceptance of our emotional selves can be more involved, as it can be hard to reason our way around our emotions. Acceptance of our emotional selves means noticing and sitting with what arises, accepting our weaknesses, our blind spots, and defences; understanding *why* we are the way we are (Are we temperamentally anxious? Were we raised by angry parents and have we learnt that anger is a way to create change in the world?); and bringing self-compassion to all parts of us. Accepting our emotional selves doesn't mean we don't continue growing emotionally and trying to live in a way that's more aligned with our values, but it does mean that we learn to accept ourselves as we are in the meantime.

> We can consider that we are doing the best we can, *and* that we can do better. This is called holding the dialectic, or tension. Yes — another excellent DBT principle.

To do this, we need to accept:

- our histories (as much as we want, we can't change what we have done or the things that have happened to us)
- our skills
- our limitations
- our finite resources (we can't have it all, or do it all)

- our psychological make-up
- the inevitability that we will fail and make mistakes
- the certainty of hard emotions and feelings.

We will all have different challenges in learning to accept our emotional selves. For some, it might be pushing against their shoulds ('I should be calmer', 'I should not be anxious'); others will instinctively avoid certain emotions and have to work quite hard to allow them in; and others will find it hard to not be self-punishing.

Before I could accept myself, I had to learn to stop comparing myself to other people and their achievements — and that was extremely hard. I was raised to be hyper-competitive, and as an adult, I found myself wanting what other people had and always finding some form of yardstick or marker to hold myself to. It felt like torture, as each achievement by another person felt like a blow, and each moment and year ticked off was a reminder of the things I hadn't done. This tendency also stopped me from forming good relationships, as I secretly played a mental game of snakes and ladders with most people I knew.

I wish I could tell you there was a magic pill that helped me shake this endless comparing of myself to others, or that might help you in whatever challenge you face in accepting yourself.

In reality, for me, it was a combination of things:

- slow therapy work (spent talking about the shame I held about myself, because really, these comparisons were all driven by a deep fear that I was not good enough)
- meditation and self-compassion practice (I love the 'RAIN of Self-Compassion' meditation by Tara Brach)
- getting older and seeing that everyone's lives take a different shape, which allowed me to realise that I wasn't defective because I didn't have or do what other people had and did; I had other things — not better, not worse, just different
- better curated social-media use (begone, foul highlights reel)
- bringing curiosity instead of competitiveness to other people
- building a values-based life that has personal meaning
- accepting some of my sorrows, failings, and disappointments — and grieving them, which allowed me to move past them.

All these strategies will apply to most of the self-acceptance battles you face.

But before any of them could have an effect, I had to get to know myself, warts and all. Getting to know yourself, as deeply as possible, is key to accepting yourself.

It's also the work of a lifetime, but to begin with, it

helps to understand the forces that made you who you are and to understand why you are wired in certain ways. Self-reflection is crucial: the capacity to think about who you are, your strengths, why you behave the way you do, your trigger points, and the ways you fail yourself and other people. This requires honesty, and the ability to tolerate knowing your weaknesses. It also requires some solitude, as we cannot reflect and know ourselves when endlessly distracted by noise and bustle. Beyond self-reflection, it may also require therapy — sometimes, despite our best efforts, we need someone else to point out the ways in which our thinking is stopping us from accepting ourselves.

It's important to remember that when radically accepting ourselves, whether our physical or emotional self, we need to be compassionate. This is not giving ourselves permission to do whatever we want. It means extending kindness, gentleness, and encouragement to ourselves, just as we would to a small child. Radical acceptance means knowing and facing our failures and personal failings and flaws, and that is only really useful if we can see them *without* punishing ourselves for them. We have to own these failings with gentle self-compassion, while still working to be kinder beings.

- If you struggle with accepting yourself, what is one simple action you can take today?
- What is one kinder, more self-compassionate thing you can say to yourself?

FURTHER READING

Women Don't Owe You Pretty – Florence Given

A fierce and fun book about body acceptance, and the patriarchal gaze.

Self-Compassion – Kristin Neff, PhD

A book by a psychologist about learning to understand and build self-compassion.

Radical Compassion: learning to love yourself and your world with the practice of RAIN – Tara Brach (also see www.tarabrach.com)

A book by a psychologist and meditation teacher, focused on building compassion for self and others.

Acceptance of others

Radical acceptance of ourselves opens the door to knowing and accepting that we are imperfect. This is vital because we spend so much of our lives trying to find some version of perfection. Interestingly, as soon as we build a strong enough practice of accepting ourselves, we usually become more accepting towards other people. This can't work in reverse — if we try to accept other people while still holding a seething bedrock of anger and hate at ourselves, we will project that anger onto other people.

I rarely speak in absolutes, but I will say that it is impossible to feel for someone else what we cannot feel for ourselves. Self-acceptance *must* accompany any other acceptance.

Acceptance of others is similar to accepting ourselves: noticing (who someone is), accepting (all of them), understanding (why they are the way they are), curiously questioning (to learn more about them), and allowing (imperfections and failures). Many of us have been raised with unrelenting standards — we expect perfection of ourselves and we project this onto other people.

Soften judgements and embrace complexity
Unrelenting standards can be the enemy of acceptance, because of the shoulds we hold in our mind (people should be politically aligned like us, people should always be kind to us). I prefer to replace these shoulds with 'it would be

ideal/nice' ('it would be nice if people were always kind to us'). This removes the expectation and allows us to tolerate it when people are not so nice.

Once again, radical acceptance of others does not mean approval of them, nor does it mean that we can't work to influence change in someone, or dislike someone, or disapprove of their behaviour, or set boundaries with them. It doesn't mean a lack of judgement — being non-judgemental all the time is hardly ideal. If we have no capacity to judge whether someone is good for us or not, we leave ourselves open to bad behaviour and mistakes. Acceptance means that we acknowledge and understand that other people will inevitably be different from us. We can accept that someone is how they are while still being self-protective and discerning. Perhaps we can even forgive them when they make a mistake.

It is easier to radically accept people if we can keep these things in mind:

- There is likely more to the story or picture than we can see.
- We will never know someone fully or understand all their motivations and emotions — these hidden forces are often what drive difficult behaviours.
- We all have a different frame of reference born of our sociopolitical milieu and upbringing. We need to make space for views different from ours (even if we disagree).
- Fundamentally, most people *are* like us in that we all want love, belonging, to feel safe, to be accepted, to find meaning.
- Radical acceptance doesn't mean tolerating bad behaviour.

A simple way to start radically accepting other people is to be curious about them. Asking questions, getting inside someone's life, and learning to see someone's full self can mean we judge them less harshly. Certain meditation practices can also help building acceptance of others, such as Buddhist loving-kindness metta meditation (a type of meditation focused on helping us see the commonality in all of humanity). Learning to reduce comparisons and noticing the internal judging voice ('I would never do that') while replacing it with something more compassionate ('That is a different choice from what I would make') can also help.

Really, many people mean well even if they express it clumsily. Starting from a place of assuming good will is essential. This doesn't stop us from looking at a person more critically and eventually deciding that they don't *actually* mean well. Assuming that we are all doing the best we can, though, might free us up to feel gentler, kinder, and more compassionate; and it might reduce some of the hurt and anger we feel.

And don't forget ... if you fail at radically accepting others, learn to radically accept *that* in yourself. It's win-win, really.

Acceptance of the world not going your way

If you live long and hard enough, you are bound to be disappointed by yourself, by other people, and by the world itself. It's important to learn to tolerate rejection, disappointment, regret, and failure without exploding in fireballs or directing anger and hate towards other people. When I work with forensic clients who harm other people, they often talk about having responded in a certain way (e.g., with violence, or by stalking), because they were let down by another person. Two wrongs never make a right, and we are not entitled to hurt someone else because they have hurt or disappointed us.

Sometimes these disappointments are broader and related to our own sorrows and regrets: the things we have not been able to experience/see/do/have. We probably all want certain things — good health, a beautiful house, people who care about us, a partner, work, hobbies, fun, travel. We may not have all these things, all the time. Some will be out of our control (such as whether we have close and connected families), while others may not click into place despite our best efforts, such as an unfulfilling search for a partner, or infertility. We may have some things, and then lose them. We may let other people down, and then feel sorrow.

I have seen people respond to these conditions in a few different ways: a desperate, unceasing attempt to find what they think they lack, with increasing anger at the world for not providing it; an absorption of identity into the longed-for thing or regretted thing ('until I find a partner, I will not be happy', 'everything would be fine if I could just get pregnant'); bitterness and anger at other people for having the thing they so want; or grief, and acceptance that the world will necessarily hold some disappointments and sadness.

When we want something we don't have, we tend to hyper-focus on it and assume that our life will be so much better with it. Realistically, we know from studies into happiness that we all have a happiness set-point, and even large and positive things (such as winning the lottery or getting married) will only temporarily increase our happiness — we will inevitably settle back into our biologically and physiologically determined grooves and will likely be the same selves we always were.

That thing you really want that will change your life? It probably won't — or, at least, not in the ways you're expecting.

We compare ourselves to people who have the thing(s) we want, and ignore the lives that do not fit in this mould. And as we focus on the things we lack, we feel worse. I am not discounting the pain of not having some cherished thing, or the fact that having certain things can add to life satisfaction. I am merely pointing out that we are all bound to be disappointed at certain turns in life and have regrets, and it is better to accept this and get on with the tasks of living (including trying to sensibly problem-solve and remedy any lacks you feel), instead of staying buried in regret, anger, and sadness.

To manage difficult times, whether personal or global, we need resilience — the capacity to tolerate disappointments and sorrows, to hold onto perseverance and hope, and to keep going.

We can increase our psychological flexibility around sadness and regrets by practising acceptance, and by recognising that we are not alone or unique in our sadness, even though it might feel like it at times. It is important not to amplify or idealise the thing(s) we want so much. Everything has pros and cons, and that much-desired thing is probably more wonderful in our heads than it is in reality, and will also bring some costs (which we usually forget to factor into our thinking).

Lacking a specific thing doesn't mean we lack the values or the emotions that may come with this goal — such as love, community, companionship, or belonging. There are numerous pathways to these emotions and values, and we can hyper-fixate on one pathway and ignore the others.

Work with what you have, not with what you lack.

If we can't fix a problem, our choice will be between acceptance or misery. I know which I would rather feel. Life is a wonderful, wandering tapestry, and it brings different people things at various points, sometimes in unpredictable ways. It is helpful to have a general map and sense of what we want, of course, but we will find greater satisfaction in the way we live our lives if we also allow for surprises and twists.

FURTHER READING

The Lonely Hunter – Aimee Lutkin

An odyssey through the trenches of modern dating, and an exploration of the cultural messages we receive about love.

Childless: a story of freedom and longing – Sian Prior

A memoir about coming to terms with childlessness and infertility.

Acceptance of death

Stick with me, I know this sounds grim, but I wouldn't have included it if it weren't important. Psychologists often talk about terror management theory (TMT). TMT addresses the fact that we all fear death. This is both understandable and realistic — existence on this earth and having a body are all we know, and not being alive anymore *is* truly scary. We also fear death for the physical pain that may accompany it, or out of concern for the people we leave behind, and sometimes because of a feeling that our life has not been well lived.

Ways to cope
We often do counterproductive things to try to protect against this fear. For instance, some people develop severe health anxiety and check their bodies constantly for new symptoms, worrying that they will develop health issues. Sometimes, the worry is not about dying but about becoming ill, which can be painful and unpleasant. Fear of illness can be about loss of control, yet more often, it also points to a deep fear of death.

Another example of counterproductive self-protection is straight-up denial. We can work very hard to avoid thinking about our deaths, but in the face of a real threat to our lives, this approach can backfire. This is one of the reasons the pandemic was so distressing for so many. Apart from potential sickness, and the economic and social losses the pandemic brought, it forced us to confront the possibility that we would die, and that we could lose people we care about, too. It's common to try to ignore these realities via a form of defensive denial; to have this denial crash down is horrifying, and can lead to a massive decline in mental health.

Accept the reality

> The reality, of course, is that we will all die, and many of us will lose people we care about before we do. In a hundred years' time, all of us will be dead (you, me, and most of the people we know — and this book will probably be out of print).

We can be terrified, or we can accept this fact and see it as freeing. When we learn to accept death as a reality, we often find that some things no longer matter as much (what we weigh, whether we get that promotion and buy a bigger house); while others start to matter a lot more (how we spend our limited days, whether we work in a meaningful job instead of amassing wealth). Suddenly, the typos I am bound to find in the printed version of this book hold less anguish.

Understand and combat the underlying fear

Acceptance of death requires a few things, including understanding what you most fear and combating that fear in some way.

I thought about this when I did a course over a decade ago at Alain de Botton's School of Life, on having a good death, and realised that most of my fears centred around not having lived fully. For others in the course, they found they feared the possible pain of illness before death, and learning more about palliative-care options and voluntary assisted dying helped settle this.

Regularly face the truth of mortality

Regularly reminding ourselves of our mortality can be helpful with managing our fear. It allows us to expose ourselves to these fearful thoughts gradually, until the fears recede. Some people find that visualising or planning their own funerals and eulogies helps (and indeed, this can be a powerful way to connect with the sort of life you want and the values you hold), while others enjoy mortality meditations.

I like to regularly remind myself that each year, an anniversary slips by unnoticed and unknown — the anniversary of the day I will die. This is not macabre and does not cause me fear or anxiety, but rather helps me reorient and check if I am living a life I like, and one that has meaning. I hope that when I do approach the end of my life, this orientation will help me die with peace, in the knowledge that I have contributed to making the world a better place, and have lived fully instead of merely stopping by.

FURTHER READING

Staring at the Sun: overcoming the terror of death – Irvin Yalom

A seminal book on understanding how death anxiety sits at the root of most of our anxieties.

Acceptance of heartbreak

When we think of heartbreak, we often think of the end of a romantic relationship. While that can cause heartbreak, many other things can also hurt us. Heartbreak is a deep sadness caused by loss or disappointment, and is a form of intense grief. It can encompass other elements, such as anticipatory grief (grief before a loss) or complicated grief (grief mixed with other emotions, such as anger or guilt). Learning to manage heartbreak means tolerating these complex emotions and placing them in the context of our lives — and noticing that to love deeply often brings the price of loss.

Learning to tolerate loss and grief is a special kind of emotional management, and requires some specific skills.

A meaningful life contains heartbreak
When I think of heartbreak, I think of my beloved greyhound, Karla. I love her madly and I know I will probably outlive her. The day I lose her will undoubtedly be the worst day of my life thus far. Nevertheless, I will not deny myself the joy of loving her deeply and dearly just to avoid that pain. Most things worth having involve a measure of pain. Relationships, friendships, the pursuit of a meaningful career, pets — heartbreak can involve temporary or permanent separations, rejections, or losses.

To have experienced something wonderful and then to lose it is painful, but so is being so self-protective that we reject joy because we fear experiencing pain.

When experiencing heartbreak, it helps to understand that the reason your heart is broken is because something mattered deeply to you, and that is a truly wonderful (and very human) thing.

Accept the pain of heartbreak

When experiencing heartbreak, we must try to allow ourselves to feel the sadness instead of rushing to feel better. Our grief may never fully go away, but if we let ourselves experience it, it will slowly grow easier. The feeling of heartbreak receding does not mean that we will forget the being we loved and lost, but it does mean that over time our emotional experiences will slowly widen out again, such that we can see and hold sadness, while other emotions and experiences also slowly slide back into view. This is a normal process and it doesn't mean you're being disloyal — it's part of the normal human grieving process.

We must learn to tolerate the painful experience of intense grief — learn to let it ebb and flow, express it, think and talk about what we have lost, and understand that we don't need to control this wild feeling. The body and brain will manage if we allow the sadness to be expressed, felt, and placed in context.

Learn and grow from heartbreak

In experiencing heartbreak and reflecting on our experience, we are allowing ourselves to decide what the meaning of that specific relationship/occurrence was for us, what we are taking from it, and how we may have grown or gained through it. Nothing in life is a failure if we can see it as part of our journey — not the whole journey — and understand in what ways we have built our wonderful selves through it.

Strategies for managing heartbreak

- Acknowledge it. Place your hand on your heart (I am a big fan of physical gestures that mirror our intentions) and say something like, 'I feel deeply sad right now, because I lost something I deeply loved.'
- Ask yourself what you might need to soothe this sadness. Allow yourself a big cry (or as many cries as you need) — heartbreak cannot be wished away.
- Hold in mind some memories or thoughts of that which you lost or were rejected from. Then try to externalise these thoughts and memories in some way, such as by talking to friends about what you lost, painting or drawing it, or writing about it.
- Find a balance between allowing the sadness but not living in the sadness. This might involve sometimes

dragging yourself out of the house for a walk, even as you are ugly crying (this is okay!).

- Reflect on the things you learnt, or how you grew and changed through the experience you had, though this is a task for later in the heartbreak process, when the initial waves of intense grief have started to settle.

- If the heartbreak involves a terminated romantic relationship (and they often do), it's important to accept the end and give yourself closure, even if the other person cannot satisfactorily tell you why it ended. Stopping communication with the other person temporarily (no social-media stalking) is very helpful, as we cannot heal while wounds are being reopened constantly.

- Ask yourself 'what now', instead of 'why' questions ('what do I do with my life now?' versus 'why did she/he/they dump me?').

- Find support in others, and in activities, that help you to feel that life is broader than one person. Our hearts *can* and *will* bear this load with some help.

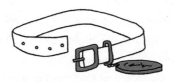

Acceptance of being disliked

Most of us want and need to belong. We used to live in tribes and were dependent on the people around us for basic survival. Things are a little different now — our colleagues (hopefully) won't kill us even if they dislike us (though they might throw us under the bus in a meeting). However, our need for connection and belonging remains the same. Decades of psychology and physiology research have shown us that social connection is vital for mental health and physical health, and that being rejected activates similar brain centres to the ones that light up when we feel physical pain. A broken heart can truly feel like a *broken* heart.

We all want approval from other people and there is nothing wrong with this. Unlike the current thrust in culture, I don't believe that seeking approval is a bad thing (no person is an island) — we just want to seek it from the right people and learn to tolerate it if the approval doesn't come.

Being disliked can be terrifying. It implies that people disapprove of us and we might be alone and exposed to danger. Many of us — especially women — have been socialised to be nice and kind, and to affiliate ourselves with others. Learning to tolerate being disliked goes against all this training. Being disliked can also bring up deep fears of defectiveness and shame ('if they don't like me, I am not good enough') and isolation ('I will be alone forever').

Learning to tolerate dislike is important for several reasons. Sometimes a fear of being disliked can stop us from living in accordance with our values and moving towards a life filled with meaning. Sometimes we also need to take a stance on things — either for our own sake or to support others — and this invites dislike. Despite our fears and pain, being disliked is almost inevitable in the large-format world we live in. We encounter so many people now, and the world is so full of information and polarised opinions that it's very likely that people will disagree with you, and even dislike you. When we learn to tolerate being disliked, we can hold better boundaries instead of rushing to people-please in the heat of conflict.

Accept that dislike is inevitable
The first part of tolerating dislike is accepting that it is inevitable at some point. Living your life trying to avoid dislike is like trying to go to the beach without getting sand on you — it might be possible, but it's the wrong thing to be focused on.

Remember this is about them, too
When tolerating dislike from others, remember that this is about them, or the dynamic between the two of you — not just about you. We would be a lot more comfortable with being disliked if we realised how much of our own inner functioning and woes we project onto other people. It is tempting to personalise and, if we are more vulnerable, to either accept and absorb dislike completely ('I must be a bad person') or reject and project ('fuck them, they are idiots').

But no more than half the relationship belongs to you, and you can't have control over, or even fully understand, another person's dislike.

Thinking about the dynamic between you is helpful, as is holding yourself accountable (e.g., if you repeatedly flout someone's boundaries, they will probably dislike you). However, some people just don't get along. This can be based on history, personality styles, unconscious expectations, or past experiences. You may not fully understand why someone dislikes you, but you *can* accept it, just as you also dislike some people. If you have wronged someone, you can make amends by apologising, but you cannot make someone like you, and should respect their decision.

Shift your focus to a broader perspective

It is helpful to keep your thinking realistic and remember that being disliked likely has little impact on your life. Most often, we can bubble along quite happily with people we dislike, still behaving in a civil and polite way. Instead of focusing on the few people who dislike you and ignoring the masses who are probably okay with you and even like you, try to turn your focus the other way. Focus on the social positives, tolerate the negatives. Don't catastrophise the outcome (having one person dislike you won't ruin your life). Ask yourself whether you will even remember it in five years' time.

Of course, if someone is actively harming, bullying, undermining, or abusing you — this is different. Disliking someone does not give us permission to behave abusively towards them.

If you find yourself in a position where you are disliked by someone who has a significant effect on your life, it is better to consider how to problem-solve or leave the situation, rather than remaining in this fraught space. Even in this situation, though, it helps to think about it practically, rather than allowing the person to influence how you think about yourself.

Dislike that's actively getting in the way of your life usually involves demonstrable, practical impacts — such as a manager who actively bullies you or blocks promotions, a treacherous frenemy who spills your secrets to all, or a family member who is abusive. Tolerable dislike usually comes from people who are not in our core circle (which means we can accept the dislike without any appreciable impacts on our lives). While we might be able to tolerate a colleague we see once a week ignoring us, if this was an immediate supervisor it would feel (and be) a lot more difficult. Some questions to ask may include:

- How close is this person to me?
- What practical and emotional impact does their dislike of me have?
- How serious are these impacts?
- Is their dislike of me influencing the way other people see me?
- Can I tolerate this dislike?

Bring it back to your values

The more strongly we are living our values-based life, the more likely it is that we will anchor ourselves against certain people. Taking a stand for the things we value means we will undoubtedly rub some people up the wrong way. This is okay, even if it feels scary. Understanding our values can help us anchor ourselves against dislike, as it helps us see it as a values clash, or as something we must tolerate in the pursuit of living a meaningful and values-aligned life. While we might still feel pain, we can place this pain within a broader context.

What if it feels like most people dislike me?

Of course, if you find that more people than not seem to dislike you or want to avoid you, perhaps this is something to address therapeutically. It doesn't mean that you are fundamentally flawed or unworthy, but it could mean that you are unconsciously playing out some harmful dynamics or that you lack social skills. All these things can be worked on. Equally, it could mean that you are in the wrong environment for you (think freshwater fish in the sea) — and might need to make some external changes.

FURTHER READING

The Courage to Be Disliked: how to free yourself, change your life and achieve real happiness —
Ichiro Kishimi & Fumitake Koga

A book using the principles of Adlerian psychology that focuses on helping people understand how to live lives free of the shackles and weight of doubts and the expectations of others.

Acceptance of not being in control

There is little that terrifies humans more than not being in control — well, except for death, of course. We in the Western world have an unprecedented level of control in our current lives. Modern medicine, the industrial and knowledge revolutions, and scientific progress have meant that we can insulate ourselves from the elements, get access to goods and knowledge at the press of a button, and change our environment in numerous ways. We don't feel vulnerable to many things, which means we are used to feeling in control of our lives.

In some ways, having this amount of control is lovely: we can steer our lives in a range of ways that have never before been available to humans. In other ways, we have forgotten that we *do* live in an uncontrollable world and that things will happen around and to us that are at least somewhat out of our control.

Much psychological distress, especially anxiety, stems from an illusory sense of control and the desperate attempts to clutch at control where there is none. When people feel anxious, they make attempts to control things. They might try to control how they present, how other people see them, or even their bodies. Some people develop disordered eating as a way of trying to control their bodies; typically, when all other means have failed.

In addition, we are increasingly called on to adapt to things we can't control: natural disasters, climate change, illness, death, other people's actions. Practising tolerating uncertainty and lack of control is vital.

Live according to the two circles of control

When working with people who struggle with control, I usually ask people to remember that there are two circles. A circle of things we can't control (the weather, other people, the global economy, climate change, our manager) and a circle of things we can control (how we plan for the weather, how we treat other people, what we do with our money, how we manage our own carbon footprint, the decision to stay in a job).

Focusing on the latter and letting go of the former can free us from unnecessary distress and lead to greater peace and the freedom to act in values-aligned ways. This works for smaller things (what to study), as well as for larger issues (climate change).

When looking at a problem, I sometimes get clients to list all the things they can't control and those they can. I then ask them to engage in actions from the list of things they can control, without being too attached to the outcome. This usually results in less anxiety and distress.

When struggling to accept things we can't control, remembering the serenity prayer can help. As a filthy heathen, I say this version to myself: 'Grant to me the serenity of mind to accept that which cannot be changed, courage to change that which can be changed, and wisdom to know one from the other.' Sometimes I throw in a sneaky amen, just because.

Acceptance of change

Change often terrifies us, perhaps because it feels uncontrollable. We make herculean efforts to avoid the unknown. Even when we expect the change in our lives and welcome it (such as when we make a life transition like parenthood), it can feel terrifying and stressful. There are probably some good evolutionary reasons why we fear change (i.e., the unknown was likely to have been dangerous), but things are different in our current world. A new job is unlikely to have a sabre-toothed tiger lurking in the office, and at worst we will not enjoy the job and will likely be able to find ways to make changes or possibly just leave. And yet, we often treat change as though serious danger lurks within it, and at times, we cause ourselves much heartache by insisting on sticking to the known and familiar, even if it isn't working well.

While change *can* feel difficult, we often make it seem even worse in the way we anticipate it. We catastrophise, imagining the change will be the worst — no good, awful — and we convince ourselves we won't cope, when we very likely will. Because of this, we can wind up feeling deeply bored or unhappy in our current situation but refusing to change it, creating a space where we feel trapped.

In truth, human beings are quite adaptable, and we will settle into any new space after a few months of adjustment, and some initial stress. The trick is to learn to use our acceptance and self-soothing skills to manage the change until we settle into it.

Techniques for tolerating change

Think about where you were five years ago. Have things changed in your life? Would you want to have stayed exactly where you were at that time for the rest of your life? For most people, the answer is no. Most people yearn for change and novelty, but also fight against it when it beckons. It can be useful to think of unexpected changes that have served you well, such as new friendships, jobs, or relationships, a new pet, or a positive change in life direction. None of these would have happened if you had clung limpet-like to the status quo.

> Change will have both positives and negatives, and there are few changes that will be catastrophic, and even fewer changes that can't be at least partly undone. When we struggle with decision-making around change, it is often because we think that a decision is final. It is helpful to remember that many decisions *can* be changed, which can reduce the pressure on us to get it right. It's also helpful to remember that when we make a choice, there's not always a clear-cut right or wrong choice. Sometimes we obsess about getting it right, forgetting that there is no objective right, just what seems best for us at that time.

Psychological flexibility

Psychological flexibility means being able to adapt and change how we think, feel, and behave in response to changing circumstances. This is a vital psychological skill; and like every other skill, it can be learnt and built upon.

Often, we have certain ideas about how things should be, or we have rigid expectations, which might mean that we struggle to adapt when life throws a spanner in the works.

Psychological inflexibility might look like sticking grimly to how you think things *should* be or having only one set of coping resources (e.g., soothing yourself by switching off through alcohol/food) — this is okay if the situation calls for that manner of behaviour, but many situations require a range of skills and ways of thinking.

> Psychological flexibility and adaptation can involve things such as changing our expectations, managing how we think about something, soothing emotion, changing communication patterns or problem-solving the situation.

For instance, if we have certain fixed ideas about how things should be in a relationship — 'all my needs should be met, my partner should know how I'm feeling, they should always support me' — then we might struggle when the reality does not align. However, if we can build some flexibility into our expectations —'sometimes my partner doesn't know what I need or can't meet my needs, but if they are generally supportive I can accept this'— and problem-solve (e.g., learn better communication skills to more effectively ask for what we want), and develop the capacity to soothe hurt emotions without blame or aggression, then we will be better placed to have a healthier and happier relationship.

Build the skill of psychological flexibility

Building psychological flexibility means *practising* this skill wherever we can in life by deliberately seeking out other ways of thinking and responding. We can start by asking ourselves daily (or even hourly) if there are other ways of thinking or responding that might be helpful in a given situation.

I like to exercise this skill by deliberately and frequently changing things up in small ways and tolerating the uncertainty that comes. Work routines, daily routines, new hobbies (especially things I'm not good at!), learning a new skill, and breaking out of my comfort zone. Faking it till you make it is fine — you may not find it easy to begin with, but we build this skill as we practise it. Over time, I've learnt to build a flexible self so I can respond to changing situations and needs without too much fuss or bother.

A few questions to build some flexibility and accept change:

- What are your expectations of this situation?
- Are you expecting perfection?
- Can you see that other people might have different expectations and views?
- If your usual way of managing things isn't working, what else can you try?
- Are there some positives in the fact that things are not exactly where you want?
- What's the worst that could really happen?

Big (good) feels

Big feels are inevitable when living a good and meaningful life. We are thinking, being, doing, and *feeling* beings; and living well requires a balance between all of these.

As we've explored, radical acceptance of emotions, understanding the meaning and utility of each emotion, and knowing how to grapple well with them as dance partners in life is a great skill.

When we think of emotions, we often think of dark and difficult emotions, and how to manage them. Sometimes we forget that we can also have and cultivate good feelings. In this section, I've focused on a few major positive emotional experiences, with a view to encouraging us all to build our capacity to lean into good feelings.

Pleasure and joy

We sometimes struggle against pleasure and joy, filling our lives instead with internal statements like 'I'll do that later, I have to work now', 'I feel guilty', 'I can't have a break until next year', or 'I am so bad for doing this!' There will always be reasons that we feel we can't access joy or pleasure, and most of these reasons are just roadblocks put up by our mind. When we focus on mental health and wellbeing, we usually think of the difficult parts of life and remedying those — reframing our thoughts, regulating emotions, working on defects. However, we have a powerful secret weapon available to us in our struggles, and we often forget to use it.

This weapon is building up the good in our lives, and learning to experience and luxuriate in positive emotions. Pleasure and joy can parachute us away from difficult things temporarily, giving us a break so that we come back renewed and reminding us that life is not all grim.

It is critical to differentiate here between toxic positivity and a more realistic appreciation of joy. Toxic positivity is the practice of ignoring difficulties and defensively insisting on being happy/thinking positively, etc. Appreciating joy in the way I encourage should still allow us to make space for the difficult — we are not denying it, but we are temporarily turning our focus towards things that enchant us instead.

Embrace pleasure and joy

To live a good life with some meaning, we need to find a balance between work and play, dark and light, difficulties and pleasure. Learning to accept and embrace pleasure and joy and to notice the small things that enhance them is an essential practice that makes this balance possible. To practise embracing pleasure and joy, we must first develop our understanding of why we need pleasure, then give ourselves permission to seek it out, and then build a detailed pleasure/joy map for ourselves of the things we love.

When I think of pleasure, I tend to focus on the small, intangible things and on recognising and appreciating their importance. This way, I don't find myself stuck on the hedonic treadmill, but can instead focus on finding joy in daily life, wherever I am. Learning to be mindful of pleasure is helpful. We must give ourselves a minute to breathe and soak it in, perhaps marking it with a whispered 'oh, isn't that nice'.

In no particular order, here are some of the things that give me an injection of Vitamin J(oy). When times are hard, I often seek more of these, to shore myself up:

* my morning coffee
* a new leaf unfurling
* rainbows
* a warm blanket and clean sheets
* weird things I see on my neighbourhood walk
* dogs in clothes
* beautiful words
* writing
* a steaming cup of mint tea
* a good yoga stretch
* a square of chocolate
* sun on my face
* a favourite soundtrack
* a good chat
* croissants with butter
* bookshops
* laughter
* the grunt my dog makes as she falls asleep
* flowers
* candles

Making a list like this for yourself means that next time you feel the world tilting too far towards the joyless, you can seek out one or more of the things that help balance it back the other way.

Can you write down your own personalised list of
the things that bring you joy, from the mundane to the
quirky? Make sure to incorporate all five senses, and
activities both large and small.

Another aspect of joy is awe. Awe is an emotion we experience when we feel connected to something much larger than ourselves and can marvel at the size and scope of the sky/the ocean/deep space/the horizon. Different things elicit awe — I most often feel it when looking at the ocean or into deep space, such as the night sky, or at NASA pictures. By deliberately seeking out experiences that remind us of the interconnectedness of life and the miracle of sentient life on this earth, we can greatly increase our joy.

What brings you joy?

When do you feel awe?

How can you make space for more joy in your life?

FURTHER READING

Wintering: the power of rest and retreat in difficult times – Katherine May

A meditation on the fallow periods of life, times when we must retreat to care for and repair ourselves.

Phosphorescence: on awe, wonder & things that sustain you when the world goes dark – Julia Baird

A beautiful exploration of the ways we can still find and pursue purpose when life is difficult.

Empathy

We often confuse empathy with sympathy, with pity, with approval, with rescuing — with all kinds of things.

When I think of empathy, I think of it as the most essential emotional competency we can have. At its most basic, empathy means having the capacity to understand and share the feelings of another. It doesn't mean we must experience *exactly* what they are experiencing — just that we can understand (to some extent) what life might be like for someone else, what has formed them into the person they are, and *why* they might behave the way they do.

> Having empathy doesn't mean having no boundaries or feeling every emotion on behalf of other people. We can feel compassion and try to understand others, while keeping in mind the difference between our experiences and theirs.

Without empathy, we might be cold and callous or struggle to understand why other people experience the world the way they do, setting us up for disappointment — or anger. Equally, without empathy we will not be able to connect with other people and will probably find ourselves lonely.

It is common to hear of people talking about themselves as 'empaths'. This word was coined to describe people who are high in empathy, but over time it has morphed, in the common vernacular, to include people who struggle to hold boundaries, who are enmeshed and co-dependent with other people, and who have forgotten that everyone is responsible for soothing and managing their own feelings.

The flip side involves people who have *no* empathy — we often call these people 'psychopaths'. There are very few true psychopaths in the world, but those that do exist can bring a world of pain to other people, as they lack the capacity to understand another's feelings and may have no qualms about inflicting pain.

How to practise empathy

Empathy is hard-wired into the human brain, but we can still exercise it.

Empathy is best exercised with self-compassion, good boundaries, and a solid psychological base. This way, we can understand our own thoughts, feelings, needs, and tendencies, and not project them onto other people. True empathy requires us to know the difference between supporting and rescuing. Empathy involves cognition (intellectually understanding how someone else thinks), emotion (feeling what someone else feels) and compassion (experiencing both cognitive and emotional empathy, and then feeling moved to help). Empathy should be a practice and a controllable skill, not something we are overwhelmed by.

Building attention and curiosity

Growing empathy means starting to expand our attention to include other people. When I focus on attuning to people as a psychologist, I start first with their bodies — what do I notice about how someone is holding themselves? Can I see any tightness, any pain, any subtle shifts? Any facial expressions? Noticing these subtle shifts is a learnt practice, and it clues me into what might be occurring inside someone. Next, I focus on what someone is saying, and on asking curious and gentle questions to understand what they are thinking and feeling. Curiosity is vital for empathy.

> A simple way of building empathy involves recognising that we all have the same psychological make-up. We all want love, and we all want to have meaning, although we may go about finding these things in different ways. Recognising our shared humanity with other people is the foundation of empathy.

Learning to ask questions with curiosity and openness is important. Some examples include:

- What was that like for you?
- Tell me more…?
- What did you think when that happened?
- How did you feel?

Learning to accept what someone says instead of arguing with them to ensure they hold the same views as we do will extend our capacity for empathy and will help the other person to trust us and open up to us.

Expand your social world

Spend time in new social circles with people who are not like you. As we spend time with people with different backgrounds and histories and get to know them, our understanding and acceptance of other people will grow, and through that — so will our empathy.

Turn towards suffering

Turn towards suffering sometimes, instead of switching off to stay comfortable. Empathy requires practice, and sometimes we need to witness suffering and act to reduce it where possible. As we allow sadness to filter through, our empathy for other people will grow.

Learn to separate when necessary

Equally, sometimes I need to turn the empathy dial down, so I can work with trauma and those who have been harmed, without being swamped by feelings myself. It's helpful to build the capacity to separate from people and hold their suffering at a distance. Without this capacity, we can't do difficult work like being a first responder, or perhaps even watch the news.

Empathy is a skill like any other, and a vital quality to have in this sometimes selfish world.

Hope

Hope is an interesting, curious little emotion. It sits at the heart of much of human endeavour, adjacent to optimism, curiosity, and exploration. We use hope as we continue to explore ways to cure cancer or engage in work designed to stop the ravages of climate change. Hope helps us tolerate difficult times and envision ways in which things might be made better. To truly effect change in our lives, we must be able to hope.

Hope carried me through some very difficult times in childhood, as I hoped that I would one day be older, in control of my life, and able to make my own decisions (I just ate cake for breakfast, so I am pleased to report that this paid off). It also carried me through my early twenties, as I hoped that I would be able to change my life and manage some of my mental health struggles. This hope allowed me to invest effort in practical things (therapy, study, creating solid friendships) that *would* create change, and this powerful combination of hope and targeted action truly *did* change my life.

Hope is closely connected to the dreams we have, and our values. We all want certain things, both simple — good friends and a job that gives us paid sick leave — or complicated — finding a way to bring more peace to the world. Hope is beautiful and multi-textured, and if we know how to use it well, it drives most change.

Hope is also intrinsic to most forms of psychotherapy; we hope that we will feel better, so we try to find help to guide us in this direction. Hope alone isn't enough, though, as psychotherapy also requires commitment to the therapy, attendance, and work during and between sessions. Hope is the first step.

Life without hope

Lack of hope can contribute to all kinds of psychological difficulties — most notably depression and lack of motivation. If we think there is no point to life, because things will never get better for us, we are unlikely to even try to make them better. This is a catch-22 — lack of effort means things *don't* change, which makes us feel even more hopeless. People with depression often get themselves stuck in these ever-widening loops of helplessness and hopelessness; and treatment often focuses on first creating small behavioural changes to disrupt this frozen state.

Building hope

> When I work with clients who feel hopeless, I work with building a sense of *existential* hope — the belief that our existence has some meaning and that things can improve and shift overall — as well as more *specific* hope, focused on smaller situations that are under our influence.

Take a long perspective

To help build this hope, I encourage people to acknowledge the broad span of human life and endeavour and the amazing things we are capable of. Being sentient and alive on this planet is a great adventure, and one that demands we honour it by believing that many seemingly impossible things are possible. We were once primordial soup and stardust — now we type on laptops and debate the meaning of life. Pretty cool.

Stay realistic

Still, we must also ensure that hope is at least somewhat realistic — blind optimism or misplaced faith does not help us much. For example, hoping that someone will recover from terminal cancer may not be helpful, but hoping that they can have a good and peaceful death is likely to be both helpful and realistic.

Use encouraging self-talk

'It's okay, keep going, most people have difficult times, things will get better'. This allows us to continue to approach difficult tasks instead of giving up.

Manage thwarted hope

Being able to manage the difficult emotions that come with thwarted hope (sadness, disappointment, cynicism) are also essential so we can tolerate these emotions and continue living a values-aligned life instead of giving up completely. Managing difficult emotion is covered in more detail in the 'Managing pointy feels' chapter.

Back hope with action

We have to support hope with concrete actions designed to get us a certain outcome. Hope is an active state, and one we can increase by *doing*. Breaking down the things we hope for into small steps can help us get started. As we learn that we can change things in our lives and increase our self-efficacy, hope can start to feel more realistic and become stronger, creating the opposite of a vicious cycle — a wonder cycle.

Boundaries and limits

Boundaries and limits are a part of living well.

While we usually think of them as something we put in place to create distance from others, they are a much bigger concept. They involve boundaries around ourselves and our resources, boundaries around relational units (such as couples or friendships), and boundaries and expectations for ourselves.

By articulating and holding boundaries, we can free ourselves up to live more fulfilling, values-aligned, and connected lives.

Setting good boundaries

Boundaries are my secret psychological superpower. I have rarely had a client who presents with any form of emotional or relational difficulty without also having difficulties setting boundaries and limits.

We have many mistaken beliefs about boundaries: that they are selfish, that we only need them with dangerous people, that they are instinctual and innate, that we can't have boundaries with those close to us, that we must have the same boundaries for everyone, that boundaries cannot change, or that other people must respect our boundaries (no one else has to respect our boundaries except us — and this means sticking to our boundaries and implementing consequences for those who disrespect them).

Why we need boundaries

Boundaries are a psychological line we draw around ourselves, and sometimes around a relational unit such as a couple or friendship. They define what our needs, limits, and capacities are and are designed to acknowledge limited resources, such as time, attention, or money. Simply put, we cannot do everything, and be everything to everyone without imploding by burning out or feeling stressed because we are trying to do too much. Poor boundaries can also leave us open to being exploited and abused by those who wish to take advantage of us. By thinking through and setting good boundaries, we can conserve energy, time, and money to do the things that matter to us, with the people who matter most. We also have boundaries around acceptable behaviours — such as not having relationships with adults who are verbally and physically aggressive to us — and we learn to flex our 'no' muscle.

> Boundaries can be beautiful. I see them as liberating, because they allow us to set ground rules for living, which then frees us up to invest in whatever gives us meaning and joy. We need boundaries and limits for other people, and we need them for ourselves.

Boundaries and limits are a core need, in fact. In the psychotherapy literature, we talk about the importance of having good limits for children while parenting. Raising children without any limits can lead to a sense of entitlement (I can do whatever I want, whenever I want) and to children who feel confused and unsafe in the world because they haven't been appropriately protected and scaffolded while they are learning. Overly harsh parenting boundaries can also have harmful effects, with children becoming

anxious about making mistakes or too risk averse. Just as children need boundaries, we need boundaries as adults in all we do and in all our relationships.

SMART boundaries

Boundaries can be confusing, so when first setting some, I find it helpful to use a SMART boundaries framework: Specific, Mutable, About You, Reasonable, and Talked About. We need to think about and articulate boundaries. While we may think they are instinctive, it's hard to articulate them clearly in the heat of the moment and thinking them through ahead of time helps us assess and create reasonable boundaries, so we can be prepared.

Good boundaries are Specific

If you cannot articulate your boundary to yourself clearly in a sentence, then it is not yet fully formed. To make a boundary specific, you need to be able to state who, what, when, and where. It's good to work out the 'why' for yourself, but you don't always need to share this.

Some examples of my specific boundaries:

- I am not available by phone after-hours to clients except in certain specific pre-arranged situations.
- I have firm policies around my therapy services, such as cancellation policies.
- I take time off work every year (even if I don't go anywhere!), and usually cap the year by taking some time off.
- I make sure I have three alcohol-free days a week.

All these boundaries (the unstated *why*) protect my time, health, and energy, allowing me to remain engaged in emotionally draining work.

Good boundaries are Mutable

Mutable boundaries are boundaries that are flexible, contextual, and person-dependent. Often, when we start to implement boundaries, we are very rigid about it and have all-or-nothing boundaries. Typically, if a boundary contains the word 'always' or 'never', it is worth asking yourself if it is too rigid. There are some notable exceptions — usually around being safe and not allowing someone to hurt you. A mutable boundary is one that considers:

* **The context** — Is the situation one that requires a different response or boundary to your usual set of boundaries? An example might be if a friend's partner is unwell, and the friend needs more support and time than you usually provide.
* **The other people involved** — How close are you to the people you have this boundary with? What are their ages? How reliant on you are they? Boundaries with children must be different from boundaries with adults, but we can still have age-appropriate boundaries with children (e.g., when I am talking to my friends, please don't interrupt).
* **Where YOU are at** — Sometimes my boundaries get tighter with certain people when I have observed recurrent patterns of boundary pushing or disrespect, and sometimes they get tighter because I am tired and need to protect my energy. Sometimes my boundaries

will become looser, based on the needs of people in my life or my own capacities. For instance, as I've said I usually have strict cancellation policies for therapy sessions. Yet I've waived cancelled-session fees for long-term clients on a few occasions — when they've locked themselves out of the house, been unexpectedly sick, or confused session timing. This allows respect for the relationship and is a carefully negotiated change to my usual boundary.

- **You don't have to have the same boundaries for all the people in your life** — Boundaries should be consistent, but there can be some flexibility based on need — of the other person and of yourself.

Good boundaries are About You

Often, people start boundary work by thinking that boundaries are about the behaviours other people can or cannot exhibit towards them. They may say things like, 'You can't ask that of me, because it crosses my boundaries.' This way of thinking about boundaries is ineffective for two simple reasons: 1. we have zero control over what other people can do, and 2. we would be crossing boundaries ourselves if we started to tell people how they should live.

A good boundary is tailored to be about you and defines limits around your energy, time, money, resources, and the behaviours you find acceptable.

Some good questions to think about as you set boundaries that are about you:

- What do I value?
- What do I want to say yes to?
- What drains me?
- What sort of behaviours make me angry or upset?
- What do I need to protect?

Good boundaries are Reasonable

Reasonable is a tricky concept to define, because the boundaries of reasonable vary from person to person and between cultures. Boundaries in collectivist cultures vary hugely from those in more individualist cultures. I am reminded of this when I meet another person of Indian origin and am very quickly asked what my parents do for work and whether I am married/have children/how much money I make within the first five minutes of acquaintance! In most Western cultures, this would be seen as very rude.

I like to use the concept of reasonable boundaries when asking something of someone, or deciding whether to say yes to a request.

Two simple questions to ask:

- Is what I am asking of them reasonable?
- Is this a reasonable request for them to make of me?

If you're struggling to define 'reasonable', seek feedback from friends or try to imagine what the average person might say.

I once had a friend who asked me to care for her children while she travelled overseas. I thought this was an unreasonable request and refused. It was outside my capacities as a (then) young single person who was both studying and working, and was a level of responsibility I did not feel equipped to take on. For me, this boundary was reasonable, and the request was not — but in a different context (such as if I were a close family member, like an aunt), the request may have been reasonable.

On the other hand, I've had friends who have asked if I can water their plants or care for their dogs while they travel (and I've asked the same of them) and these requests are reasonable because they account for each other's needs, are not too resource or responsibility heavy, and are skills within my wheelhouse.

Good boundaries are Talked About

Talking about boundaries could mean they have been negotiated within a relationship, or it could mean they have been expressed to those they are relevant to. If you don't tell someone else what boundaries you have, then they are left guessing, and expectations and wires (and boundaries) can remain crossed. Of course, we don't start relationships by announcing our boundaries, but a good relationship should allow space for organic conversations about them. Simple statements such as 'hey, I didn't like it when you teased me in front of your friends' can start these conversations.

Setting boundaries and limits for ourselves

When considering boundaries, we need to think about limits we place around ourselves in various domains, including work, intimate relationships, close friendships, acquaintanceships, dating, and family. It is as vital to have some boundaries, and to draw on our healthy, adult parts to support ourselves in setting limits. Some of our these limits might be related to a healthy lifestyle (I will not spend all day in bed unless I am really tired; I will not drink every day), emotional wellbeing (I will invest money in therapy and practice my skills between sessions), or relationships (I will notice if someone appears to be too unavailable and will not pursue a relationship with them).

FURTHER READING

Set Boundaries, Find Peace: a guide to reclaiming yourself – Nedra Glover Tawwab

An excellent book focused on helping you understand and create boundaries.

Helping other people without drowning

This book is predicated on caring for oneself and caring for others, so it will not surprise you to know that caring for other people is a value I hold dear, as is contributing to community. Almost everyone has a helping role in some capacity (i.e., as a parent, child, or friend), and some of us also hold these roles professionally.

> For good mental wellbeing, it is essential to have strong boundaries around any caring role we have, whether professionally or personally.

Attempting to help other people without boundaries can lead to exhaustion, carer burnout, and, eventually, compassion fatigue and apathy. Boundaries in helping mean reflecting on questions such as *why* we help (i.e., what personal value does this link to), *who* we help, *when* we help, and when we *can't* help. As I covered in the previous chapter on setting boundaries, we have finite resources and must create some firm limits for ourselves.

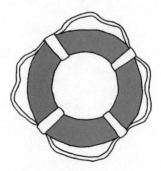

Finding the right reasons for wanting to help

People can feel obliged to help and/or rescue other people for various reasons, both positive and otherwise. Sometimes we want to help because we've been conditioned to be a people-pleaser, or we feel the pressure of social norms (such as gender attitudes around women being helpful and kind), or we want to feel needed, or we have difficulties saying no. Helping can feel good, and we can get a buzz from the gratitude people show. But none of these reasons are sufficient. To truly be of service, we should try and help because helping is linked to a personal value, and to the change we want to see in the world.

> We can't help everyone, and we can't fight for every cause — we *must* make some choices.

Support others to be responsible

Helping wisely includes making sure we help when we can, but that we do not rescue. Rescuing means doing so much for other people that we take away their personal responsibility. Outside certain situations, such as caring for a child, we may support other people by helping them, but responsibility for their lives and change should stay with them.

I tell my therapy clients that they should treat me like a driving instructor. I sit beside them, guide their driving route, and look for danger, but I don't drive for them. This is a useful framework with which to approach most caring roles.

Know when and how to say no

Helping means knowing how much we can offer, and when and how to say no. We will inevitably let people down at times or fail to meet their needs, and we have to accept this. We will all feel fatigue at times in caring roles, and we must carve out time for ourselves and know when to take a step back. Sometimes we need to exercise self-compassion and give ourselves permission to care for ourselves *first*. Helping is often an ultra-marathon, and rest breaks are essential, including scheduled self-care time and holidays. There are few caring roles we can't exit temporarily (yes, even parenthood) and we will be better able to care for people once we have had a break.

Helping well also means recognising that we can't commit to everything at once. This might involve some soul-searching, as we decide which charity we want to volunteer for, or some hard learning, such as the first time we have to say no to an overly dependent family member or let someone make a mistake that we can clearly see coming.

Some questions I ask myself when deciding whether to help include:

- Is this a commitment that fits my current values and goals?
- Do I have the capacity to help?
- Do I have the time?
- What else do I have on?
- What will the cost be to me?
- Do I truly want to help, or do I feel beholden?
- How can I tolerate the feelings of guilt or disappointment that come up when I can't help?

Most commitments don't require all these questions — dropping a close friend off for a medical appointment is often just 'can I juggle this around work?' — but the bigger the commitment, the more questions I ask myself before saying yes, and the more likely I am to put boundaries around it.

Being able to help well also means understanding when my desire to help is driven by the wrong motivation, and understanding when I am no longer being helpful and need to withdraw.

It's hard to know how to say no to commitments. Saying yes is easy and enjoyable for many of us, but saying no requires that we risk displeasure or conflict. A daunting task, but one made easier with practice. A range of simple scripts might help:

- 'I'd love to help, but unfortunately, I don't have capacity.'
- 'I'm sorry, but that's a no from me.'
- 'That's something I can't commit to at this time, unfortunately.'

Don't fall into the trap of over-explaining or apologising too much.

I've found that people usually respond well when you say no. If people push back or ignore what you've said, you might have to reiterate what you've already said ('as I said, I can't help with that').

Withdraw from helping commitments if you need to

I often find I need to tweak my commitments — the nature of my work and my tendency towards self-sacrifice means I often find myself over-committed and exhausted. I try to set myself some rules I *must* adhere to (such as writing no more than one book at a time), as well as regularly reviewing my commitments. I also remind myself that other people are around to help, too — it isn't only up to me. Sometimes this means I have to say no to something I've previously agreed to do. I've found that most people don't care as much about these changes as I do — it's my own inner dialogue about being unreliable or failing that I have to push against.

Review your helping commitments

* What are some areas of helping you want to pull back from?
* Are there areas you want to extend into?
* What boundaries will help you support other people in a sustainable way?
* How will you enforce and revisit these boundaries?

A note on allyship

The words ally and allyship are used a lot. This refers to uniting oneself with another (person, cause, group) to further common interests or aims. It is often used in social justice circles to describe people who may not belong to a certain group (such as the disability or LGBTIQA+ communities) but still wish to support them. Allyship is recognising that certain communities have faced disenfranchisement and historical difficulties, and doing your part to support them in their struggles to achieve equity.

Make a deeper effort with a specific group

Allyship is a helping role like any other and it requires the same boundaries, including careful consideration of how and who we ally with given the time, attention, and resource commitments we have. Choosing not to ally with a group or cause doesn't mean we are nasty to that group, of course — we can be kind, respectful, informed, and focused on equity without having a specific allied role.

> Being a good ally means we need to have special knowledge of a certain set of issues, and this can take time and effort to develop. There are fine-grained delineations in each situation.

For instance, working on racial equity may mean understanding the diverse needs of Aboriginal Australians, African Americans, Rohingya Muslims, Hazaras from Afghanistan, and Dalits from India. The group you ally with will often be determined by geographical considerations and your own background. We can't lump all people of colour or from different backgrounds into a single category and use a one-size-fits-all approach. Building knowledge of the distinctions and nuances of an issue requires time and a deep dive. It also includes active learning and work, not just cursory social media posts.

Forgo performative allyship in favour of informed action
I often see allyship used in a performative way, which is helpful for no one. Equally, allyship does not mean attacking other people who make mistakes on social media (I personally call that ally*shit*). If you feel strongly about an issue, then take steps to engage with a community, learn and read widely first, and take direct action guided by the community you are allying with. No community needs a saviour. Work with a community, not for a community, and do things that truly make a difference (such as learning to listen to other voices, reading literature, attending rallies, writing about things that matter, or donating). Focus on communities, but also on seeing the real people within those communities.

Use your privilege for good
Agonising over your own privilege isn't helpful. No disenfranchised group has the time or capacity to notice or care about other people's emotions about their privilege. It's better to own what you have, be aware of the hand you hold, enjoy the hand you hold, and use it for good in whatever way you can.

FURTHER READING

Help for the Helper — Babette Rothschild
A stellar book focused on supporting therapists and those in helping professions and roles to manage and navigate compassion fatigue, vicarious traumatisation, and stress.

Balancing rights and responsibilities

We all have certain rights. Most of us were born into societies that enshrine some of these rights in law (such as the right to free speech, or to dignity and respect). Other rights are assumed, based on the social norms around us. In Australia, we assume a right to socialised, affordable medical care based on the health system we have. We might also assume other things: the right to feel heard in our families, to feel safe with friends, to be able to spend our money as we wish. All of these are fair rights to assume we have, and to desire from life, and they are rights we have implicitly given and built for each other. I have, however, noticed an increased focus on assuming that we have rights *without* thinking about the rights of others.

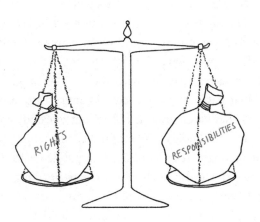

The social contract we have (i.e., the unspoken agreement we sign up to as a member of a society, a family, a group, a nation, and the broader global community) assumes that the rights we have apply to everyone, equally. What this means is that for our rights to continue to function, we have to exercise our social responsibility to ensure that other people have the same rights we do. Our rights are only intact as long as we can trust our society to uphold them — if we all focused only on our rights and ignored our responsibilities, society would be in catastrophic freefall.

As a member of a group, our responsibilities might involve not physically harming someone else, respecting other people's property, and protecting other people's health (such as by getting vaccinated against a communicable disease, or getting regular STI checks if we are sexually active).

Focusing only on our own rights can leave us angry and distressed. We might react with anger if someone tells us to put our dog back on leash, because we believe we have a right to enjoy our walk. However, if we remember that other people also have the right to enjoy their walk, and could have a reactive dog with them — we might understand their perspective and feel less angry. Similarly, when we think that vaccination is only about our body and what goes into our bodies, we might become angry about a vaccine mandate. If we consider that public health is about protecting the health of all, which means breaking chains of transmission (i.e., it's *really* not just 'my body, my choice'), we might be less angered by a vaccine mandate.

For a functioning society and for a better relationship

with the community around us, we must learn to balance our sense of entitlement to our rights by asking ourselves what our responsibilities are, and what the rights of other people are. Doing so can lead to better and more enduring relationships, and a calmer life.

Some helpful questions to guide your thinking:

- What are my rights in this situation?
- What about other people's rights?
- What responsibilities do I have? How do I balance these?

Self-care

The term 'self-care' originated in the social justice movement and initially referred to acts that members of marginalised communities could do to provide mental and physical health support to each other that they were unable to access through other sources.

The definition of the term has changed dramatically since then, and reading or hearing about self-care these days often sets my teeth on edge. The concept is overused, has been seized upon by those wanting to sell us things, and has taken on the anodyne connotations of soothing oneself when life feels hard by lighting a candle or having a bath. There is little conception of community care, or of people taking care of each other, when we talk of self-care. Nor is there a focus on more radical acts of self-care, such as setting up lifestyles that can endure, both for ourselves and the planet.

Changing your life as self-care

When I hear the term 'self-care' now, it's usually in the context of extremely burnt-out clients asking me what they can do to make themselves feel better. My answer is usually that the self-care they need means an overhaul of their life, to ensure that they have a more meaningful and sustainable lifestyle. Bubble baths and spa days are adjunctive acts of self-care to a well-formulated life, but *cannot* compensate for being constantly frazzled and over-committed. Expecting that kind of self-care to change your life is like popping an aspirin for a broken leg.

When I think of self-care, I think of self-acceptance and self-compassion first. To truly care for ourselves, we need to see ourselves as human beings, not human *doings*, who are enough, who are worthy, and who deserve a good life filled with joy, meaning, calm, and connection. Additional components include working on providing and receiving care from other people, and embedding ourselves in community, and ensuring that we have enough time and energy available for these close connections.

This approach can encourage people to rethink their focus on achievement and the belief that they need to tick off certain lifestyle goals, and to instead try to work out what really fulfils them. I don't want to dissuade people from achievement. Reaching goals can be wonderful, and having a drive to do something meaningful is amazing, but it is hollow unless it operates within a manageable lifestyle. Burnout means you won't achieve what you want anyway, so better to slow down well before the rubber rips against the road.

Self-care primarily means good limit-setting for oneself and learning to make conscious choices about what we will and won't do. As we exercise these skills, we become better at making choices that are about caring for ourselves.

- We learn to commit to something although it feels unpleasant at the time (a degree, exercise) because we know it has meaning.
- We learn to allow some people close, and form stronger boundaries with others.
- We learn to turn off social media so we can do some work.
- We learn to unplug from work and plug into a holiday.
- We learn not to use alcohol as our sole means of relaxation.
- We learn to recognise when certain systems/ organisations are exploitative, and then take our money and selves elsewhere.

These are all acts of self-care and building a good life, a life that has rhythms of work and rest.

Some more good practices for self-care
Work regular hours

If your work regularly needs huge amounts of overtime as some professions do (I'm looking at you, medicine and law), make sure that you have the temperament you need to sustain this lifestyle. If you don't (and that's not a failing!), then explore other ways to work in your chosen profession without sacrificing yourself and your health, or consider working part-time.

Don't check email or answer phone calls from work outside work hours (this is difficult, I know!)

Communicate this loudly to whoever needs to know, and stick to this boundary. I know you likely think that you are indispensable, and that work will fall apart without you (we all do), but there has *never* been a single system that has ground to a halt because one person temporarily stops working. If work protests your limits, that speaks to bad boundaries and poor management on their part, and may be a sign you should think of finding a new workplace. Voting with your feet has power when it comes to changing systems.

Use your paid time off well

Plan regular vacations (I try to have time off at least three times a year, even if I stay home) and remember that personal days can be used for rest and mental health, as well as for physical sickness. Prevention is often far easier than a cure. Join the union if your workplace doesn't allow for this time off. Agitate for unionisation if you don't have one.

Plan your week and annual cycles with a good balance of rest and activity

Times of high intensity should be followed by a physical stress-discharge activity (such as a yoga class or massage) and a period of lower-intensity work. Weekends should be used to rest, decompress, and rejuvenate (which can involve fun activities, of course) instead of using them to catch up on endless socialising or self-improvement that you feel you *should* do. You may have a range of ideas around how you should use your weekends/time off (Go to a party, because everyone else is? Use it for something productive like a side hustle?). I encourage you to examine these unspoken shoulds, and to instead commit to rest, play, and recovery.

Learn to understand your own temperament and how to work with it, rather than against it

Are you anxious? Do you need more rest? More socialising? I need significant periods of solitude and sensory rest after a day of providing therapy or being otherwise busy — if I don't give myself this, I get tired, crabby, depressed, and life feels grim. Self-care to manage this *does* involve things such as dim lighting and lovely candles, but above all it means I need to know myself, accept myself, and *listen to myself* without guilt or thoughts like 'why can't I be social, everyone else goes out after work'.

Plan self-care

Having spoken disparagingly about candles and bubble-baths, I nonetheless urge you to learn to care for yourself regularly, in the loveliest ways you can — as if you are a darling, gentle, tender infant. Having a suite of regular self-care activities you schedule can be soul-filling and provide you with anticipation. Feeling anticipation is a primary positive emotion for humans, and much of the joy in things like vacations includes building that sense of looking-forward-to.

Some things I do for my regular self-care involve: time with friends, regular meals, eight hours of sleep a night, burning nice candles, going to a bathhouse, dropping off social media, using warm blankets, brewing good herbal teas, drinking beautiful glasses of wine, walks in nature, walks with my dog, a cheeseboard, massages, road trips, writing group, yoga classes, book club, and an hour spent reading in bed each night. I don't do all of these at once, of course.

What investments can you make in yourself?

Community care

As a reminder: we can't speak of self-care without talking about community care. This goes back to the original meaning of self-care and the concept of a community caring for its own — both giving and receiving. I write about this with caution, as those most likely to take this concept on board are those who are caring by nature and are already probably burnt out from performing other caring roles; mothers, health professionals, social workers, therapists — often women. Community care involves giving to your community, but it also means knowing when to ask for care from other people and allowing yourself to receive it.

There is no shame in need, and we have done ourselves great harm by buying into the notion that being needy is bad. In truth, we all need nurturance from other people, and we all need good systems around us. Don't be afraid to ask regularly, to allow yourself to receive (some help, a compliment, pleasure, a kindness, support), and to squawk your need from the rooftops. Don't be afraid to give generously, too. Giving from a full(ish) cup can itself be a beautiful act of everyone-care. But don't even *try* to pour from an empty one.

Let's be real

This world can be a confusing place at times, with contradictory feelings and pieces of information. It's easy to be pulled in multiple directions at once and to feel like it is difficult to know where to begin, or how to filter information.

In this section, we will explore ways to keep it real, including understanding (mis)information, and learning to orient oneself towards helpful realism, instead of toxic positivity.

Realism, not optimism

Positivity has been sold as a miracle cure for mental and physical health distress, as a way to manage most conundrums, and as an essential way of being in the world. It is common to hear or be told 'just be positive' when experiencing difficulties or feeling down. Most of us *do* have a negativity bias through which we filter in the negatives and out the positives — once we recognise this, it can help us notice the positive and lift our mood. But thinking positively is rarely beneficial on its own, and it can seem dismissive of the hurt or anguish someone is experiencing to urge them to 'just be positive'.

Some examples of positive thinking I often hear, and especially dislike, are:

Everything happens for a reason.
No, many things are entirely random, and we often have no control over what happens to us, or why these things happen. We did not attract misfortune. We cannot solve misfortune through positive thinking and manifestation.

It's going to work out fine.
We can't know that it will be fine, but we can know that we likely have — or can build — the resources to manage whatever happens.

It could be worse.
It could, but it could also be better. How about, 'things are bad and feel difficult right now', instead?

> *At least it isn't as bad as X, Y, Z. I can't complain.*
> An invisible trauma measurement scale doesn't help us
> do anything except pile guilt on top of whatever difficult
> emotion we're already experiencing.

Focusing on being positive has several drawbacks. It can be (or can feel) invalidating in the face of distress, it can stop us acknowledging and soothing our own feelings, it hampers the development of empathy, and it can lead to poor relationships characterised by dismissiveness. It also stops us problem-solving. In total, it is often a form of emotional avoidance.

Negativity and positivity are often presented as the two ways of being in the world. Either you're a Pollyanna, trying to always find happiness wherever you are, or you're dour and grim — always focused on what might go wrong, or what is difficult.

There is a third way of being, and one I much prefer. This third way is the path of realism: of trying to see reality for what it is, without needing to skew our thinking towards positive *or* negative. Being realistic still requires that we acknowledge our inherent negativity bias (we tend to focus on the negative as a way of protecting ourselves from danger) and course-correct slightly, but without veering into positivity.

> Realism asks that we look at a situation from all angles,
> look at the pros and cons, acknowledge *all* feelings and
> soothe the difficult ones, and then act based on what
> needs to be done.

To build our capacity for realism, we can ask ourselves a few questions:

- What are the positives and negatives of this situation?
- Am I weighing one side more than the other?
- What's the other side to this story?
- Could things be worse? Could things be better?
- Am I discounting any perspectives, or any emotions?
- What is the most balanced way I could see this?
- Am I responding with emotion and discounting logic?
- How can I tolerate this reality?

Understanding good information management and combating disinformation

When I was studying my honours year in psychology, I was forced to study an egregiously boring subject on the philosophy of science. I remember feeling so resentful that I had to learn about the philosophical basis of science and logic when I just wanted to study psychology.

Now, I am grateful for this subject as the topics it covered (understanding how science formed, how it evolves, why it is sometimes wrong, how to argue a point well, how to test and disprove theories, how to understand my own biased thinking) are essential to the work I do as a psychologist, and as a writer.

The spread of disinformation

We have so much information available at our fingertips now, and not all of it is real. The idea of 'fake news' is widespread, and widely understood, but we forget that other information can be fake, too — images, scientific studies (such as the falsified data stating that vaccines cause autism), health information, social and political information. Even if information *isn't* fake, we use it incorrectly and struggle to understand it. We often think we understand and know more than we do.

> Having no knowledge can be dangerous, but having a little knowledge is *very* dangerous, because we don't know enough to know the limits of that knowledge.

Understanding and managing data and information is vital for living well and responsibly in society, and is intrinsically linked to good mental health. If we get information about mental health from social-media wellness influencers, we're unlikely to be getting good-quality information. Similarly, medical information from charlatans can stop us from seeking appropriate and timely treatment; it could make us sick, or even kill us. At its extreme, false and biased information leads to the spread of conspiracy theories and the radicalisation of people. Understanding information and how it can be abused can stop us from falling down ideological rabbit holes designed to play on our emotions, and save us much anger and anguish.

How to practise good information management
When trying to understand information and disinformation, I follow a few principles that were drilled into me during my psychology training.

Understand that all information can be twisted for benefit and gain
Looking for information from multiple sources (such as a few different news sites) is the best way of managing this. Some sources (Fox News in the US, Sky News in Australia) are particularly biased, and will almost always spin information in a certain way. Similarly, other sources are set

up to shock and entertain. Any information on social media can be faked, and is rarely a good source, unless shared by a trustworthy organisation.

Seek out high-quality information from experts, and watch for conflicts of interest

Information differs in quality. High-quality information is based on actual research, and published by people who have no vested or hidden interests beyond researching/examining a certain area. It is usually published in places like peer-reviewed journals or government websites. While these journals are not accessible to many of us, and can be complex to understand, we can find good science, cultural, and political writers who translate this information for us — sources like the BBC, National Geographic, the ABC, *The Guardian*, and *The Atlantic* have high-quality journalism underpinned by fact-checking, and I tend to trust them. Look for conflicts of interest (such as a study funded by a certain pharmaceutical company). These conflicts of interest may happen, but good researchers state them openly and avoid them where possible.

Good information is usually produced by experts who have training in their field. I find it problematic when people with no mental health training talk about concepts like ADHD and trauma. Many people feel they have an instinctive grasp of these subjects, but without training or knowledge of the complexities of work in this area, they fall into traps of over-simplification and misinformation. There is a difference between people speaking about their personal experiences and reporting on what other people are researching (which is fine), versus giving advice to other people (not so fine).

Google or background check your sources of information
Don't be afraid to google people (and check if their degrees are real — you can buy degrees online!), and give more credence to information provided by people with real degree-level qualifications in their field.

Understand that changing advice does not discredit the source, especially in scientific fields.

Certain fields like medicine move very quickly, and information is often being updated and disconfirmed. This is why health information changes — it doesn't mean the initial advice was wrong, but rather that the scientists have done the ethical thing and changed their advice based on what the science shows.

Learn to recognise logical biases
Logical biases are flaws in the ways we argue. Things such as attacking a person to discredit them, red herrings (statements that are not linked to an argument but send someone down a different path), and cherry-picking information (only presenting certain pieces of information and discarding others) are signs of clumsy and biased thinking. If I see these flaws, I tend to discount the information being provided by the source, or I look up other sources to confirm.

Limit and tailor your news consumption
Building good information-consumption habits can save us a world of pain. If we can find a few sources to trust and only look at them sometimes and in-depth, we avoid the constant bombardment of (often bad) news that overwhelms us. I suggest that people have one news channel and a few

online/print sources they trust, and only engage with news and media at certain preset times. I also encourage people to check information they find on social media and check primary sources (i.e., where the information came from) if something seems odd or overstated.

Accept the limits of your own knowledge and be open to new information or perspectives

We sometimes fall into the trap of thinking we are experts at things ourselves (such as epidemiology during the pandemic). Combating disinformation includes knowing the limits of our knowledge and accepting that we will never know everything. It also means being able to graciously accept a different view and course-correct. Some good scripts for this moment are:

- 'Wow, that has made me think of things in a different light.'
- 'Now that I have this information, I will need to reconsider my opinion.'
- 'I forgot to account for this, and have changed my mind.'
- 'I was wrong.'

I like to fact-check the limits of my own knowledge. I find an article on a certain topic (such as immunology) in a peer-reviewed journal (Google Scholar is good for this) and read the whole thing. If I don't understand it, the statistics behind it, or the terms or techniques used in it — then I determine that I am not an expert and should shut up and leave the job to people who know what they are doing. Simplistic, but it works.

FURTHER READING

What Is This Thing Called Science? – Alan Chalmers

An introduction to the philosophy of science, and general principles underpinning the scientific method.

Bad Science – Ben Goldacre

A hilarious and informative book focused on exploring the bad science that surrounds us in the media and advertising.

A Survival Guide to the Misinformation Age: scientific habits of mind – David J. Helfand

A book focused on helping people develop an understanding of how to use information, and scientific habits of mind.

Embrace differences and embrace the grey

Most of us will fall into lazy habits of thinking at times — a common example is black-and-white or polarised thinking. We expect neat binaries (such as good or bad) and we view the world through this lens, always looking for simple answers. This is fine when the questions are easy, such as 'which movie should I watch', but less helpful when the questions are more complex or when arguments can be made either way.

Some complex questions without neat answers:

- Is becoming vegan the right thing to do?
- When do my rights impact on another's rights?
- Am I entitled to express my views if they hurt someone else?
- How do I balance boundaries with providing care for others?
- What can I do about climate change, while still doing some of the things I enjoy?

Many of the issues we grapple with are complicated and require us to articulate our personal value systems and ethics, and take a deep dive into knowledge in certain areas.

Considering veganism, for example, requires knowing your personal ethical stance around animal rights, sustainability, and health, some awareness of sustainable farming practices, and consideration of the needs and rights of others — like children or animals in your care. It might also require an understanding of food insecurity and poverty, and the needs of people in developing countries — so we don't project our privileged views onto people with far fewer nutritional options than we have.

The cost of black-and-white thinking

At times, we engage in this automatically, while at others, it's the easier and less emotionally fraught option. Believing that things are right or wrong, that people are good or bad, or that issues are simple may bring peace — but this is often illusory. It also comes at a cost, as we force ourselves to quickly choose one option over another or feel outrage and contempt for those who make different choices.

Learning to embrace differences in people, and the grey in most choices, means accepting that the world is not neat — there are as many views and ways of being as there

are people, and many of them are adaptive and helpful, even as they're different from our ways of being. When we recognise this we feel less outrage, and often have greater psychological flexibility and compassion for ourselves and others. Resisting the urge to box in ourselves, or others, will help us live in the world in a different way.

Learn to think in dualities

DBT is built on managing dialectics (or the tension) between two poles. One of the dualities it supplies are:

> People are doing the best they can.
> *and*
> People can do better.

I held these both in mind during the early stages of the pandemic, and it helped me respond with compassion to the fear, anger, and terror I saw — and supported me with tolerating when people made different choices to mine. It probably didn't change anything external, but it helped me access peace at a time I was already on emotional overload, and it kept me accountable for behaving in the best way I could — when I desperately just wanted to rant.

Some helpful questions to ask yourself:

- Could this thing be true *and* this other thing also be true?
- Are there alternate ways of seeing this?
- What biases am I bringing?
- How does my upbringing colour how I see this?
- How would someone else see this?

How to know when you have enough (and why this is essential)

Not knowing when you have enough can distress you in a few ways. You might keep comparing yourself with those who have more than you. You might work to the point of exhaustion or worry compulsively about how much you have versus what you think you *should* have. These comparisons are poisonous and leave you feeling locked into a perpetual game of snakes and ladders.

The pressure to have more
The systems we live in are in disarray, and many people have limited access to the basic things they need to live well, while others abuse systems of power and maintain a single-minded focus on hoarding resources for themselves and their dynasties. This imbalance causes a lot of psychological distress.

Of course, we need money, and we need *enough* money — but structures built *only* around money and profit-making for *some* people are doomed to fail the rest of us. I am not advocating for us all to move off-grid and stop working entirely. At this point, we live in a capitalist society, and I — as much as anyone else — like to have nice things. I buy clothes (sometimes too many), I travel, I drive an unreasonably large car, and I work to afford these things. Modern life necessitates some of these things, and others are choices I make for pleasure.

I merely suggest that we carefully question *how much*

we buy into capitalism and the relentless push to do better, grow bigger, and acquire more. A continued focus on always increasing the profit margin of a business, monetising each hobby, or feeling like we *have to* climb a corporate ladder — these are symptoms of our drive for toxic growth. Nothing can grow forever, and it's better for us (and the planet) to learn when we have achieved the threshold we are comfortable with, and then work to consolidate.

The emphasis on more comes at huge planetary and personal cost, as we work so hard, often burning out in the process, to make money that we may not need. It also comes at cost to others, as the more we accumulate and hoard, the fewer resources (such as housing) there are for other people. We've been handed a Faustian bargain.

We know that after a certain point, the wealth we possess provides diminishing returns. Once you have enough to have the basics for a good life, collecting more will not make you much more content. Most of us forget this basic research-based psychological truth, especially as we live in a system that deifies having more, having bigger, having newer. We often buy as a way of fulfilling our psychological needs. If we want comfort but don't have the words to know that, then maybe that expensive candle will bring us some peace.

Refocusing on enough

Learning to identify when we have enough is an essential part of good living. This allows us to make choices based on our values instead of constant financial pressure, and frees up time to spend on hobbies and with people we love, as well as allowing us to sleep and rest more.

There is no rule of thumb for identifying enough — everyone has different needs and lifestyle preferences, but it's important to ask ourselves a few basic questions:

- What does a reasonable lifestyle look like?
- Have we experienced lifestyle creep, meaning that the more we've earnt, the more our lifestyle has changed, requiring us to keep working harder to maintain it?
- What is a need versus a want?
- Could we be happier with a little less? An apartment instead of a house; a local holiday instead of an overseas trip? I like using the Swedish concept of 'lagom' here (i.e., just enough) and will sometimes tell myself 'that's enough, stop now' when I reach my satiety point, whether with food, purchases, or experiences. There's a tipping point at which too much becomes unpalatable, and learning this point is a skill.

Unconscious and unspoken pressure to keep up with a peer group, insecurities and worries about not having enough or being left to fend for oneself (money is often seen as a buffer against vulnerability), and deep-seated difficulties around money or entitlement to resources also contribute to the struggle to stop striving for more.

Money won't sustain you on a dead planet, and you

won't take any money or belongings with you when you die.

Think about the impact consumerism, capitalism, and the pressure to live, look, and behave a certain way have on your mental wellbeing. At best, it might exert a slight tug and sway you away from your values. At worst, you might be completely burnt out and exhausted by trying to maintain your lifestyle, trapped on a hedonic and consumerist tread-mill as a way of soothing yourself, further perpetuating your need to keep working so hard.

We all have different lifestyles and needs, so it's hard to provide a one-size-fits-all perspective. Nevertheless, there are some things to ask yourself to help you decide what is enough for you.

- What are your core physical needs? What do you need to meet those needs?
- What's non-negotiable for you?
- What does each new thing you have, buy, or do cost? Not just in terms of money, but in terms of time and planetary resources?

- What trade-offs are you making between time, energy, and money?
- At which point do you feel like you will have enough, or have arrived at the lifestyle you want? How sustainable is this lifestyle — for the planet, and for your own energy levels and capacities?

You have choices. Use them wisely. What is one small change you can make today to help you get off the treadmill?

You don't have to rethink everything, protest capitalism, quit your job, or move into a commune. Small values-driven actions — saying yes only to certain things, resting instead of side-hustling, stopping to think before hitting buy, not using shopping to self-soothe, not upgrading your car yet — can be enough to drive lasting and sustainable change, while still allowing you to live and partake fully in this wild and wonderful world.

Let's take action

Identifying what we want from life and learning
to ensure that we build realistic and helpful
thinking patterns, and can manage emotion,
are critical skills. Once we have these core
skills in place, it can be helpful to think more
broadly about how to change and influence
specific aspects of your life and the lives
of others around you.

In this section, we will look at a few action-
oriented skills designed to help us make
changes to our own lives, or the socio-
political milieu we reside in.

Build self-efficacy and good habits

'But I just can't find the motivation' is one of the most frequent complaints I hear, both in my private clinical psychology practice and from people I encounter in my daily life. It is a common lament of those with serious mental illnesses (such as a depressive episode, where lack of motivation is a symptom) but also of people who struggle with a lack of get-up-and-go.

I have worked with people who want to work harder, study more, exercise more, develop a new hobby, or commit to a new business idea, but struggle with building the momentum they need. They think about doing things, but find themselves procrastinating, or never commencing an activity, despite their best intentions. I have been in this place, too.

Feeling that you don't have motivation and can't get things done can be very distressing. It can leave you feeling bored and dissatisfied, unable to change things, helpless and trapped. To live a good life, we need to be able to get meaningful things done.

Forming habits instead of waiting for motivation
I now get past lack of motivation in a simple way — by ignoring it completely.

When I want to do something (write this book, finish a degree, exercise more), I focus on understanding *why* I want to do it, what value or goal it hooks into, and I go about systematising the steps involved so that working on the task becomes a habit. This could mean writing for an hour daily (even if I hate what I have written and delete it all) or booking in yoga classes at the same time each week.

> I don't wait for motivation, or the perfect system, to do things I value, just as I don't wait for motivation to brush my teeth. I do the latter, twice a day, every day.

I still have off days, of course, and sometimes cancel a gym class or decide not to write; but these days are far fewer than they would be if I only worked when I felt motivated or inspired. Approaching life in this manner has also helped me build a strong sense of self-efficacy.

I often suggest that my clients try to build habits instead of waiting for motivation to strike, and those who can adopt this philosophy usually have more success with forming and adhering to commitments and better mental wellbeing than those who continue to wait for that elusive motivation.

Rules for forming habits

Decide whether you can commit to forming a new habit

Everything has an opportunity cost. Each hour you spend working is an hour taken away from sleep, learning, exercise, friends, and recreation. Everything you commit to has a cost. The world is drowning in productivity information and exhortations to do more, but the wisest thing you can do sometimes is to decide that you don't *want* to do more. Doing less, and doing wisely is a better orientation.

Keep it simple, start small, and be regular

The best new habits are those that are achievable. You are unlikely to commit to a new exercise routine that takes an hour a day, but may be able to walk for 15 minutes, three times a week. It may not seem like much, but it is a lot more than nothing. Habits build over time, and you can increase the amount of time/energy you commit to something once you've established your initial baseline. It is better to only try to form one new habit at a time, to avoid overwhelming yourself.

Chain habits

It is much easier to commit to a new habit if you link it to something you already do. For example, practise Duolingo while you wait for your coffee to brew, or meditate for five minutes straight after breakfast.

Evaluate

It's okay to start a new habit/routine and realise that it isn't serving you in the way you hoped. Set aside time to re-evaluate habits and routines regularly, and give yourself permission to change things that are not satisfying.

Accept that you're good enough

Ever felt like you were not good enough? Hands up, people with the imposter syndrome in the back.

Most of us have felt this at various times, especially when being evaluated, in new situations, or in high-stakes spaces. For some people, worries about not being good enough pass quickly, but others struggle, and get stuck in loops of anxiety, low self-esteem, and attempts to compensate for the deep-seated worry that they are inadequate in some way. Each attempt at compensation might bring momentary relief ('maybe if I win this prize, I am actually okay'), until the next challenge beckons.

Several thoughts can reinforce this sense of defectiveness. Do any of these resonate?

- 'I must be good at something before I try it. If I'm not good at it, I'm a failure.'
- 'If it isn't perfect, there's no point.'
- 'If I don't know as much as everyone else, I'm failing.'
- 'If I don't know the answer to a question, it's because I'm stupid. I have to pretend I know.'
- 'If I think I won't be good, I just won't go.'

These thoughts and avoidance behaviours are designed to keep us from confronting our deep fear that we are not enough. However, each time we give in to the thought that we need to be perfect or keep trying harder, and that failure/weakness/imperfection are Very Bad Things Indeed, to be avoided at all costs — we strengthen these tendencies.

The way past this is through this.

The origins of 'good enough'

Good enough is a time-honoured psychological tradition. The term was first coined by D.W. Winnicott about parenting. He noted that a parent needs to be good enough (i.e., to be sensitive, attuned, available, and flexible), not perfect. Anyone who has had a newborn will know that their rhythms and needs change quickly, often from moment to moment, and that pushing for perfection can lead to difficulties in responding to an infant's needs and annoyance/anxiety when a baby can't be soothed or ignores their routine (as is inevitable).

Abandon perfection

The first step is to change our goalpost from perfection to good enough. In most cases (not you, surgeons), good enough will suffice.

Good enough means we turn up, give things our best, try hard, and accept the outcome. It means we won't always get it right, and that sometimes we'll have to say we don't know. It means we can accept trying new things that we aren't good at, and that we can tolerate being silly, and can laugh at ourselves. It means we can cut ourselves some slack, learn to honour our need for rest and breaks, and can go with the flow.

Practise being good enough

With this is mind, ask yourself if are there areas of your life within which you aim for perfection. How would being good enough instead be beneficial? What would it look like?

The next step in moving away from perfection is to start enacting the behaviours associated with being imperfect but good enough, and tolerating the anxiety that arises. It will feel scary initially, but that's okay — anxiety is only an emotion. Good enough is a muscle, and we build it by doing.

Here are some things to try:

- Say 'I don't know, I'll need to look it up' instead of pretending you have the answer.
- Notice thoughts like 'I can't do it, I won't be good enough' and replace them with 'I'm here to learn, not to be good at this'.
- Do something you are bad at.
- Try a new hobby.
- Read a genre you are unfamiliar with.
- Try a new physical activity (an excellent way of accessing some of these embodied patterns).

Practise forgiving yourself

In the above examples, and anything else you attempt, bring self-compassion instead of judgement when you fail, and try to redefine your expectations of yourself.

Can you forgive yourself when you make a mistake, and perhaps even learn to celebrate a failure, or a time when you were good enough?

Some of the most experienced psychologists I know can openly acknowledge fallibility and own it when they either don't know something or are unsure of how to help a client. This is a good model for clients and early-career colleagues, as it allows exploration. In contrast, most beginning psychologists find this incredibly terrifying and quickly run to the surety of *some* kind of response, even if it's not the best answer for that client. Sometimes, it's good to sit in the not-knowing.

> Good enough is a powerful mindset with which to approach the world. It encourages self-compassion, psychological flexibility, and confidence. No one is perfect, and we posture (or strive) for this at our own peril. Good enough allows us to take action — to try things and strive for things that we would never dare if we felt we had to be perfect. The opportunities for making meaning that come with this new ability to act are invaluable.

Learning to resist

We cannot make change in the world unless we learn to resist. We might want greater gender or racial equality, fairer working conditions, equitable access to abortion and healthcare, or better funded disability care. This is not an exhaustive list, and we will each have our own priorities.

When thinking about resistance, my mind turns immediately to the idea of anger.

Anger gets a bad rap. People think it is dangerous and fear it, or confuse it with aggression or violence. Anger is an emotion, like any other, and it serves a protective function. It tells us when things are wrong and pushes us to take action. To resist, we often need to be angry first.

Lots of things make me angry: the sexualisation of women, Donald Trump, anti-vaxxers and science deniers, Twitter, trolls, conspiracy theorists, greyhound racers. Some of these I can manage by avoidance because I know I can't change them (Twitter, Trump, trolls); with others I feel inspired to do more.

When we get angry, we need to know how to take action. This is resistance. Without it, we might sit with simmering anger with no outlet, feeling increasingly resentful and trapped or despairing. Resistance gives us agency and self-efficacy. If we don't resist, nothing changes; for us or for other people.

What is resistance?

Resistance is the act of refusing to accept or comply with something. It has also been defined as group opposition to the political, economic, or social actions and policies of a government or society. Ideally — both are important. Merging acts of personal resistance and group and political action is vital. I see resistance as values-aligned action in favour of greater equity and fairness.

I am lucky to live in a democratic and open society, and resistance for me means making my own choices around how I live, writing about things I think are unfair, donating money, and volunteering. Other people I know are politically involved and have joined environmental organisations, support not-for-profits, sign petitions, and march in rallies. Some go against the law in the pursuit of meaningful action, such as those who protest native forest logging and environmental causes despite increasingly draconian punishments. People in other countries have often had to take firmer stances, have worked underground in unfavourable political climates, have protested, and have even gone to prison or been killed in pursuit of resistance. Resistance can be fraught, and whistleblowers and protesters are often punished — though they do extremely important work.

To resist effectively and safely, we need to have a framework for why and how we do it.

Interrogate why we are resisting

The why is, in one sense, easy — we resist because we want to effect some change when things are unjust. But determining whether things truly are unjust is important, as we can sometimes be self-justifying in our entitlement to access things.

I am *not* of the school that accepts and encourages all emotions and wants as valid (no, this is *not* my job as a psychologist). The anger that groups like incels (involuntary celibates) direct towards women, for instance, is odious, and I would never support them resisting what they consider to be an unfair distribution of sex. Nor did I support the anti-vaccination marches I saw at the height of the pandemic. These were acts of short-sighted resistance, based on poor science education and an individualistic focus on rights, with a complete negation of social *responsibilities*.

Before resisting, seek some corrective feedback from people around you (including people who can *disconfirm* your beliefs) and think carefully about whether your stance aligns with the general principles of fairness and the balance between rights and responsibilities (see the earlier chapter on this). We cannot rely on social norms alone for this checking process, as societies have often been unfair and wrong (such as the views we have previously held about homosexuality, or women voting).

The most valuable resistance will grow from being fully informed about an issue (not through social media alone), and being led by current thinking in a field.

Resist effectively

If resistance feels beneficial, and values-aligned, then it's time to think through *how* to resist effectively. In general, I support resisting within the paradigm of the law, and only in ways that do not negate your responsibilities. Choosing not to pay taxes is not resistance; it's more often self-interested evasion. There *are* times when more radical action is called for, such as when our rights are being systematically eroded, or when we live under corrupt or harmful regimes.

Speak out (face-to-face)

Speaking out on unfair issues is important, but we need to know how best to do this. Resistance doesn't give us the right to abuse someone else. It should typically be directed at structures, rather than individuals. We may need to address individual actions as part of this (e.g., I tell people when I think they have said something sexist or racist) but we can do so respectfully, without abuse or (too much) self-righteousness. These conversations are best had face-to-face. Many issues are complicated. People may feel morally pure and self-righteous, but the world is rarely clear-cut. Navigating these conversations is tricky, and — especially when conducted on social media — I have seen these conversations degenerate into free-for-alls, with each party feeling abused and retreating defensively into entrenched views. No one learns from being shamed; at best, they might acquiesce.

I also don't find much utility in being a warrior on social media. It can feel more like virtue-signalling in an echo chamber, and more lowest-possible-effort than meaningful action. That said, for those who have the energy and can manage the trolls (not me) it can be a useful tool. Use it as a tool, though, not the whole armoury, and back it up with some form of direct action. When led to say something publicly, I ask myself these questions:

- Has this already been said?
- Do I need to add my voice to this issue?
- If I do say something, how likely is it that the person receiving it will feel attacked?
- How can I say this respectfully? (The answer to the latter is almost never 'in 140 characters or less'.)
- How can I acknowledge someone else's view before presenting mine?

Having some specific scripts to know how to address things can be helpful:

- 'I understand that you were coming from a good place, but what you said felt like it was demeaning/harassing/objectifying (etc).'
- 'When you said X, I felt Y.'
- 'I acknowledge your point, but this is how I see it.'
- 'I wonder if you realised that your statement might be perceived as quite hurtful to some? This is why.'

I avoid phrases like 'educate yourself', and 'do better' (especially when directed at people) because they make people defensive, which means that the conversation won't progress.

Addressing things directly will probably lead to push-back; everyone can get defensive if they feel like they are being called out. Before getting involved in a back-and-forth dialogue, consider whether someone sounds receptive or defensive, and whether they'll become further entrenched in their views. Sometimes making a statement and then letting people go away and mull over what you've said can be much more beneficial in terms of longer-term behavioural or attitudinal change than bludgeoning someone with your views.

Remember that we are rarely completely correct, and our views will inevitably change with time. Social norms change, language changes, views change; we will all likely look back at some of the things we have believed, done, and said with horror.

> Acknowledge compassion as an essential part of resistance and recognise that no one is perfect. Give yourself grace and give other people grace.

Resist with personal choices and direct action

Specific actions will be led by the needs of the issue you are working on but may involve things as simple as voting (don't discount this!), refusing to support a business that underpays staff (and letting them know why), writing letters to the editor, making formal complaints, or volunteering for organisations. Every tiny piece of direct action counts, and making personal choices *and* engaging in collective action is immensely powerful.

Speaking up is also important. While I've addressed social-media 'call outs' above, we *can* use our words directly to address harms. Letting things slide for politeness' sake or to keep the peace means things won't change. And yes, you might get called an angry woman/man/person — welcome to the club!

Notice when you need to take a break

Sometimes resistance may feel like too much and we might need a break. If you are experiencing constant anger at the injustices in the world, feel fatigued, find that you dislike other people more than usual — you might be exhausted by the fight and be experiencing compassion fatigue. If so, put the burden down, and step away briefly. It is a marathon — not a sprint.

A note on social media and trolls

Social media is rife with bullies and trolls. It's made up of easy and anonymous platforms that allow people to quickly form and share strong views, with no personal accountability. Humans tend to cluster in groups, and it's easy for an online mob to form. It may feel like words can't hurt, and there's no one behind the screen. There always is, and words *can* hurt, sometimes even driving people to suicide. When using social media, I always moderate my words, and tackle issues rather than people. Of course, there are exceptions, and if people place themselves in the public eye and endorse hate speech, the right of response is fair, but should *always* be proportionate to the initial offence.

When managing trolls, cyberbullies, or a pile-on on social media, I use a few principles.

- Allow the level of exposure you feel comfortable with and remember that accounts can be private.
- Don't argue with the bad-faith reader, or the person who wants to tear you down. Block instead, and move on. It's best not to get stuck in endless cycles of defending yourself, justification, or explanation if someone feels determined to take offence — it's rare for these efforts to change the mind of this sort of person.
- At some stage, people will take offence to something you say and will troll you or perhaps try to de-platform you. I know many writers are terrified of this, but I've had to accept that this will probably happen to me because of my strong (and sometimes unpopular) views. I've found some peace in accepting this as part of the zeitgeist of the age, and prefer to work with publishers who have the backbone for difficult discussions.
- Don't set yourself up as a paragon of virtue or as someone who always gets it right. If you do make a mistake or say something ill-informed or stupid, apologise and move on. If you hold well-researched/ well-formulated/evidence-based views (even if they are unpopular), stand firm and don't be bullied into submission by possibly well-meaning but ill-informed words. You will never please everyone. Use social media and your words carefully, and set yourself the task of thinking before you speak or share.

Managing burnout

Burnout is something we are talking about a lot for good reason. We have lived through a pandemic, and many of us are working longer and harder than ever before. We were exhausted before the pandemic, and now we are even more exhausted. This is not down to personal failure but reflects the increased demands on many of us — home-schooling, working from home, lack of social contact, working within overstretched systems — all these things have impacts on the people caught in the systems. Some of these things have reverted to normal now, but their effects over several years can't be dispelled so easily.

Burnout is a complex phenomenon. It is not just 'tiredness'. The concept was first described in the context of human services professionals who deal with other people's problems. At its core, it is physical and mental exhaustion, detachment from one's work, cynicism (negative attitudes towards work or life), depersonalisation and dehumanisation (seeing the other as not quite real or human), and a poor sense of effectiveness at work. We use the term 'burnout' in a much broader way now, and it's easy to understand why when we look at the scale of the problems surrounding us.

We are thinking and feeling beings, and our burnout reflects workplace tiredness, but also cynicism, worry, and a sense of despair and dread at the large-scale social, economic, environmental, and political problems we see. The personal demands on us, and the failure of the socio-political structures around us have collided, somewhat catastrophically.

In the context of work, burnout often occurs due to systemic failures and under-resourcing. Sometimes, when systems fail, demands are transferred to individuals. As an example, it's becoming increasingly common for doctors and nurses to be required to work without leave. This has largely happened because of decades of underfunding of health systems and inadequate staffing levels. Health practitioners are expected to sacrifice themselves for the greater good, and very long shifts and many hours of over-time are the norm. Systems benefit from the desire to make a difference most health workers have, and the self-sacrificial tendencies people hold.

It's easier to move pressure downward, onto individuals, rather than upwards, to those who have created and implemented policies and been responsible for ensuring sustainable resourcing.

Unsurprisingly, many individuals caught in these systems are burnt out as they try to compensate for these systemic failures.

When confronted with these issues, I like to ask myself two simple questions:

- Is this a me problem?
- Is this within my pay grade?

A 'me problem' is something within the scope of my responsibility, such as how I attend to my clients, working to deadlines, and ensuring I have the right training and knowledge. An example of a 'not me' problem is something outside my circle of control, like whether my organisation has enough staffing to complete the work it has tendered for, or whether there are enough psychologists in the country to meet the needs of all Australians. Working within my pay grade is a similar concept. It doesn't involve callous dismissal or a refusal to do any tasks that are outside my role, but does involve careful consideration of my capacities, an understanding of limits, and prioritisation of my life over my work, as well as the ability and willingness to send problems back up the chain of command, and push back on unreasonable demands.

Managing burnout is an essential skill for longevity in the mental health profession. I realise that it may sound unfeeling to limit my focus, but holding this orientation allows me to feel and care very deeply for the clients I have, so I can keep working with people who need help for a long time. It also means I must tolerate knowing that there are people who need help but can't access it, and the moral distress that arises, as well as the possibility that people may dislike me when I refuse to play ball with their demands.

Look for the cause of burnout

Managing burnout requires creative and deep thinking. Are you exhausted because you are doing too much and expecting that you can have it all? Cynical, because your work requires you to enforce laws and rules you fundamentally disagree with? Apathetic, because you have tried to effect change for years and feel like giving up? Distressed, because your hard work is not proving enough to pay the rent? Overworked, because your manager is forcing you to pick up the work of all the other employees who have resigned? All these types of distress have different roots and require different solutions.

Sometimes we haven't really looked at how we are feeling in more detail beyond noticing that we are 'busy' or 'tired'. Busy and tired are such common words that they are now almost meaningless, and there's often a host of feelings and experiences behind them. Consider whether busy really means 'doing too much', or 'not enough rest', or 'can't make a difference in the ways I want', or 'my job feels meaningless', or 'I don't know how to say no and am always behind'.

Managing burnout includes understanding and acknowledging it as a form of emotional distress, and a signal that significant change is needed — instead of quickly trying to shift it so we can go back to our normal tasks.

Understanding burnout *can* be distressing, because it sometimes forces us to confront parts of our lives that need radical action. But the effort to understand it is essential to help us live a good life. We can contribute to changing bigger social problems, but we're not responsible for fixing everything for everyone.

Sometimes, even if we see things are falling apart, we have to allow it to happen.

Pre-empt burnout

I love my work as a psychologist and find it immensely meaningful, but it is also extremely tiring. Sitting with other people's difficulties all day exacts a slowly creeping emotional toll. I work to pre-emptively manage burnout by carving out chunks of time for myself and by seeking restoration in supportive and caring structures (such as personal therapy, yoga, regular holidays, and time with close friends) — but I also know that I may not be able to be a psychologist forever, and certainly don't have the temperament to do face-to-face client work five days a week.

Finding roles with a balance between client time and non–client time, and considering carefully the settings I can tolerate working in, helps me extend my longevity in the role. I would rather work less and work longer than go too hard and quit in a few years in a blaze of flame. This also means that sometimes I can't do types of work I value (such as working with people who are in prison), because of the personal toll the setting takes on me.

It might be useful for you to spend some time assessing your work and commitments in a similar way. Planning ahead is the one of the best ways to stave off burnout.

Managing burnout also requires changes in the life structures that cause the burnout.

Some helpful questions to consider when contemplating how to pre-empt or manage burnout are:

- How do you feel?
- What else do you feel?
  What ELSE do you feel?
- What is making you feel this way?
- What else is making you feel this way? (And keep asking yourself this question …)
- What shifts do you need, to address the things making you feel this way?
- Are these shifts practical, emotional, or cognitive?
- Can anyone else support you with these shifts?
- What discomfort will you need to tolerate to make these shifts?
- What feels sustainable in terms of a long-term lifestyle you want?
- What sacrifices will you need to make? (And there will always be sacrifices.)
- How can you challenge the fallacy of arrival, i.e., once I do X (retire, get promoted, pay off the mortgage), *then* I can rest.
- Is your work encouraging you to sacrifice yourself? How sustainable is this?
- How much unpaid labour are you doing? Why?
- Are you taking on problems that are not yours to solve?

Things that help

- time off work
- scheduled vacations
- unplanned or planned mental health days (mental health is health too!)
- taking leave without pay
- working less
- working shorter shifts
- working in roles that don't involve shiftwork
- working in non-client-facing roles
- a change of role entirely
- working for an organisation that cares about staff
- a new hobby
- stopping a side hustle and working on non-monetised hobbies instead
- moving closer to work
- moving a little further from work
- turning your phone off
- getting a pet
- a self-compassion practice
- nature
- feeding yourself well
- yoga classes
- eating the rich (sorry)
- eating a little snack in bed (not sorry)
- being up high somewhere
- exploring something weird, wonderful, and woolly that reminds you that the world is pretty cool
- pausing activism
- joining a union
- saying no

- caring for your body
- learning to receive
- art
- boundaries
- asking for help with childcare
- not being a perfect parent or a perfect anything
- screaming
- stopping that one after-school sport/hobby
- remembering you can't change everything
- reading something wonderful and wise
- bee-keeping
- gardening
- swimming in the ocean
- making music
- and just being present to this wonderful world *outside* the need to make money or achieve.

You might find that *you* are the biggest obstacle to making changes. Making a change in lifestyle, or committing to rest, requires resistance against shoulds and finding ways to allay any anxieties that come up ('if I stop working for a few months, will people forget about me?').

FURTHER READING

Burnout: the secret to unlocking the stress cycle – Amelia and Emily Nagoski

A simple, science-based plan to help women minimise stress, manage emotions, and live a more joyful life focused on understanding and ameliorating the factors that lead to burnout in women.

The End of Burnout: why work drains us and how to build better lives – Jonathon Malesic

A fascinating first-person and journalistic exploration of the history of work, the ideals and ideas we have about our work, and the manner in which social factors push us towards burnout.

Pulling it all together

I realise that I've thrown a lot of information at you, and you might be feeling flustered, confused, or overwhelmed by the thought of where to start. It might be tempting to avoid the distress of confusion, to ignore this book, and return to life as normal.

We *do* know, though, that life as normal is broken. It cracked open a long time before the pandemic, though the pandemic exposed all the cracks in our social systems and the poly-crisis within which we live.

It's time to start making some changes.

While the world is in a difficult place, this is not very different to where we have been at other times in history — with looming wars, pestilence, and climatic events. Each generation has worried about the state of the world, and while the worries we have right now are huge and scary, we have the capacity to make huge change, both for ourselves and for generations to come. The human race has endured many difficult things, and will likely continue to endure and adapt. Our challenge is to ensure that we can shape this adaptation fruitfully and gently, so that our continued survival does not come at the cost of the planet and its flora and fauna, and so that we can continue to encourage the best parts of humanity (courage, adaptability, hope, intelligence, kindness) while minimising the worst (greed, selfishness, hostility).

The best place to start with change is right where you are, and with some hope that you can slowly start to change yourself, and through that — the world.

Remember that the skills I've provided here have taken me over 15 years to learn and implement, and that I keep working at them daily (and often fail!). Mental wellbeing is not something that can be built in a day. There is no magic pill.

There's no perfect way to approach change, but you *can* start paying attention to yourself, your body, and your instinctive sense of knowing. Did something I said especially jump out at you? Does your mind keep returning to a line? Pay attention to this. Pick one skill, and decide on an action you can take today, or this week, to start building it. Add on another skill the week after (always with an emphasis on self-compassion, and being just good enough).

Making changes in the world doesn't require big actions. Really, we are just shifting towards a slightly smaller world. Less stuff, a simpler and slower life, fewer expectations. Over time, these simple actions can revolutionise the way you feel about yourself — and they can also change the world.

Acknowledgements

Marika, a huge thank you for taking a punt on this book based on a chat over pho, and a one-paragraph email pitch. You're such a fabulous person to have in my corner, and I feel truly lucky to be able to work with you, and have deep respect for your ethical stance, consideration, care, compassion, editorial vision (and your tolerance for my spiteful gremlin humour and *seriously* snarky asides during edits and writers' festivals). You're the Sam Kerr of publishing.

Anna Thwaites, thank you for the excellent and sensible edits that gave this book more clarity and shape.

David Golding, for proofreading — while your best work is always invisible to others, I am very grateful for your careful eye and assistance with rounding out the corners of this book.

Laura Thomas, thank you for giving my words such a lovely skin; and Angi Thomas, thanks for the lovely illustrations. Cora, Tace, Josh, Marina, Chris G, Sarina, Alice, Chris B, at Scribe, as always, thank you. I recognise and value the immense work you all do behind the scenes to get my books out there and into people's hands ... and other author's books into mine!

On a personal front, thank you to all the usual suspects for your support of me, especially as I navigated the chaos of debut book release last year, and your tolerance as I disappeared for weeks at a time because of 'book shit'.

The three people/beings this book is dedicated to — you all have certain qualities I hold in high esteem, and I am grateful to be anchored by your care. Karla — you are sassy, have soft ears, a juicy nose and beautiful-smelling feet (undervalued qualities), give exactly zero fucks about smol yapping dogs (a true lesson for us all), and are a self-care KWEEN (put yourself to bed at 6.30 and lick your bum whenever you want, you star). Snigdha — you have such a big and beautiful heart, so much care for others, and such a smart mind. Love being your sister. I'm still taller, though. Steph — your resilience this year has left me in awe. You taught me how to stick out difficulties and communicate instead of running, and I'm so grateful to have your wise mind and insightful and deep reflective capacities to draw on. Glad I wet you.

Thank you also to all the commissioning editors, writers' festival programmers, fellow authors, panel moderators, reviewers, podcast hosts, journalists, and booksellers for your support as I entered the world of being an author.

And finally — thank you to all my clients. I learn as much from you, as you (hopefully!) do from me. Your successes and joys gladden and lift me, and I value the trust you place in me.